ANGER AND RELAPSE:
BREAKING THE CYCLE

Anger and Relapse: Breaking the Cycle

JO CLANCY, LMSW-ACP, LCDC

PSYCHOSOCIAL PRESS
MADISON, CONNECTICUT

Library of Congress Cataloging-in-Publication Data

Clancy, Jo.
    Anger and relapse : breaking the cycle / Jo Clancy.
        p.   cm.
    Includes bibliographical references.
    ISBN 1-887841-05-9
    1. Anger. 2. Aggressiveness (Psychology)   3. Control (Psychology)
I. Title.
BF575.A5C57   1997
152.4'7—DC21   96-53387
                                                                      CIP

Manufactured in the United States of America

Contents

Acknowledgments   vii
Preface   ix

Part 1: Plotting a Course

  1. Identifying Key Players   3
  2. Reactions and Responses   11
  3. The Patches on Your Quilt   21
  4. Kerosene and Campfires   29

Part 2: Blueprints for Recovery

  5. Turning Down Your Thermostat   45
  6. Mind Games   53
  7. Which Way Does Your Lava Flow?   63
  8. Generating Options   87
  9. Balancing Your Boundaries   109
10. The Elastic in Your Underwear   125
11. Life's Too Short   145
12. Beware of Exploding Potatoes   159

Part 3: Learning How to Fly

13. When You Roller-Skate You Get Skinned Knees   179
14. What About the Twelve Steps?   187

Epilogue   197
Suggested Reading List   201

Acknowledgments

To Jay Sonkin, Ph.D., Michael Durphy, M.D., and Jeanne Deschner whose 1985 edition of *Learning to Live without Violence: A Handbook for Men* and 1984 edition of *The Hitting Habit: Anger Control for Battering Couples*, respectively, served as primary resources for this book. Special thanks are also extended to Terence Gorski and Merlene Miller whose book *Staying Sober: A Guide for Relapse Prevention* (1986) and subsequent client manual *The Staying Sober Workbook* (Gorski, 1989, rev. 1992) provide a frame of reference for the anger–relapse cycle. I am also indebted to Kevin Grillo whose computer skills brought the drawings and models presented in this book and in my first book *Anger and Addiction: Breaking the Relapse Cycle* (1996) to life.

To my husband Vinny whose tolerance of my moodiness and exhaustion from writing on Sundays and into the wee hours of the morning provided the anchor of stability I needed to make this book a reality. Without his enduring love and patience I would have abandoned this project before it began. To my son "Vincent the invincible" for providing the stress relief that only a 3-year-old can create. And finally, to my mother and sister, who make me feel like a winner no matter what. Your support helps me endure the challenging task of juggling family, career, and my passion for writing.

Special thanks to Ed, Frank, Burl, Roger, Don, David, Sam, and the hundreds of other clients who have and will participate in the anger management/relapse prevention training program. This book, as promised, is for you. I hope it helps you maintain the life changes you strive so hard to achieve and hold onto. Each of you has a special place in my heart and are living proof that the human spirit can and does rise above adversity when challenged.

Preface

This book is for real people; the men and women who struggle daily to better understand and more successfully navigate this journey called life. You will learn to identify patterns of anger that time after time fuel your return to addictive behavior. You will also learn to recognize triggers and cues, put anger management skills into action, and maintain new behaviors across time. Most important, you will learn that ending the anger–relapse cycle can only happen when the pain of current life circumstances is greater than your fear of change. This is an intervention model I practice as well as teach and it works— *if* you are willing to encounter the person behind the mask of anger. Good luck with your recovery!

Part 1

Plotting a Course

1

Identifying Key Players

Traveling is one of my favorite ways to spend a vacation. It gives me a chance to see new sights and spend time with my family. It also helps me escape from the realities of everyday life! I recently took a trip to Cozumel, Mexico with my husband and family. It was great—we lay on the beach, ate lots of fish and lobster, and the most challenging thing I did all week was read a mystery novel. Sounds like a dream, right? Well, getting ready for this trip was some kind of work! As a family we had to decide how much money we could afford to spend, when to go, and how long to be gone. We considered where we had already been, and where we wanted to go this year. We had to order airline tickets, arrange for our hotel, make arrangements for transfers to and from the airport, exchange dollars for pesos, pack everything we needed for a week, locate our passports, make arrangements for our 3-year-old son, arrange for others to see our patients for a week (my husband is also a social worker)—the list goes on. I was so tired at one point I wished I was Samantha Stephens on *Bewitched*—just twitch your nose and you're there! I also thought about *Star Trek*—just set those coordinates, step on the transport pad, and poof—you're in Mexico! Unfortunately, since I'm neither a witch nor a treckie, planning this trip required a lot of hard work!

When you think about life in general, just about anything we do that is meaningful takes a lot of time and effort up front. If you buy a house you have to decide how much you can spend on a mortgage, what area of the country you want to live in, explore schools for your children, research the job market, make arrangements to move your belongings. When furthering your education you have to decide what to study, identify sources of funding, arrange your schedule so you can still meet other obligations, and research the job market (is there a demand for this type of skill). When you get married you have to set a date, make arrangements for the service, reserve a reception hall, order food, hire a photographer, plan a guest list. In other words, the most important things in our lives require a lot of planning and hard work!

Plotting a course for recovery also requires advance planning. You have to consider who can help you, how and where to find help, and the types of interventions that best suit your needs. You must also consider the length of time different phases of recovery might take. As with trip planning, it is important to review where you have been, where you are now, how you got there, and where you hope to end up. By exploring these factors, you greatly increase the likelihood of achieving long-term, quality recovery.

This chapter marks the first step in plotting your course. Key players: anger, addiction, relapse, and recovery, and their role in the anger relapse cycle, will be defined. Subsequent chapters will refine your course by teaching you to recognize factors that activate the anger relapse cycle, introducing coping skills to redirect your responses, and identifying strategies to help you sustain new responses across time.

We can begin this process by reviewing some definitions of anger. If I asked you to describe anger, many of you would say, "It's when someone yells and curses or makes hostile gestures (shoots the finger, shakes a fist, jumps up and down, or gets in your face)." Others might describe anger as a seething rage that runs just beneath the surface and keeps everyone walking on eggshells. These definitions describe different ways in which anger can be displayed, but it is equally important to identify factors that create anger reactions.

Two important ingredients in the anger reaction are fear and pain. Human beings are, after all, animals. When we are afraid or in pain, our survival instinct kicks into overdrive. Our primary goal becomes staying alive and in one piece regardless of the consequences. Once activated, survival instincts cause us to react without thinking. This is a highly effective tool in life-threatening situations (combat, physical attacks) but can create serious problems in everyday life. Survival instincts produce intense emotional reactions that interfere with decision making. Because our ability to decide what is harmful versus helpful is often distorted by fear and pain, we may take aggressive action unnecessarily—often with negative results. For example, say I experience a back injury and am in terrible pain. I am also very frightened (i.e., fearful I will die or be permanently disabled). If a good Samaritan tries to move me, I may lash out in anger. This reaction, driven by pain and fear, is activated by my belief (if you move me, I'll be paralyzed or die). Although my goal is self-preservation, my aggressive reaction becomes a barrier to the help I so desperately need.

Anger, simply defined, is an emotional state that exists on a continuum ranging from mild irritation to intense rage. An individual's location on this continuum at given points is greatly influenced by his or her expectations about how the world should function. For example, my mother taught me to wash pots and pans as I use them when cooking so the kitchen is clean when I finish preparing the meal. My husband stacks up all the pots when he cooks and cleans up after the meal has been prepared and eaten. If I try to apply my expectation about cooking to my husband, I might become very angry. If, on the other hand, I choose to *modify my expectation*, admitting that although we do it differently, the end result is the same, my risk of becoming angry is very small.

I believe anger reactions involve a *combination* of factors whose interaction leads to a wide range of response choices. When we are confronted by something that *appears* threatening or frustrating, instinctive changes in our body functions (increased heart rate, sweating, more rapid breathing, turning red), plus changes in mood (whether we feel sad, scared, angry, confused), plus changes in thinking (how we define what is happening), ultimately result in a specific behavioral response (how we choose to respond: yelling, hitting, walking away, trying to explain our feelings). Further discussion of this approach will follow in chapters 2, 3, and 4.

Addiction is another key player in the anger relapse cycle. Definitions of this term have changed dramatically in the last 50 years. Prior to the 1960s addiction was generally viewed as an issue of morality. People defined alcoholics and drug addicts as disgusting, weak, immoral individuals who refused to stop living self-destructive lives. They received little sympathy from the general population and even less from the medical profession. In the 1960s, thanks to the work of many dedicated researchers, addiction was recognized as a legitimate medical illness. This reclassification of alcoholism and substance abuse as diseases promoted the belief that some individuals are born with differences in brain chemistry that place them at higher risk for addiction than are others.

Additional research indicated that once susceptible individuals abuse substances, further episodes of abuse are reinforced by their beliefs and expectations about the effects alcohol and drug consumption might produce. This combination of genetic influence and environment means that medical treatment alone is not enough to generate lasting change. Early detection, followed by interventions to generate changes in thoughts, feelings, attitudes, and life-style are necessary to control the disease process. If an individual has high blood pressure and is placed on a medication to regulate it, but they continue to eat fatty foods, drink alcohol, smoke, and avoid exercise, the medication will be only partly successful in achieving the desired result (normal blood pressure and reduced risk of heart attack and stroke). Likewise, if an individual stops drinking or using drugs but does not alter who they associate with, where they spend their time, how they cope with stressful events, and how they manage thoughts and feelings, they will undoubtedly return to active substance abuse.

An example will help demonstrate this concept. Imagine a display of dominoes carefully arranged to create an elaborate design. Does it *really* matter if I knock down just one little domino? If it is the *last* domino in the display it probably doesn't, but what if it is any other domino? The innocent act of knocking down one domino creates a chain reaction that results in the destruction of the entire display. Addiction creates an identical chain reaction: Once set in motion, it affects parents, siblings, children, coworkers, friends, neighbors, the taxpayers who must pay for medical care when affected individuals get sick or injured due to substance abuse, or legal fees to finance the court system that prosecutes them when they drink or drug in public or behind the wheel, and so on. The simple act of taking the first drink, toke, snort, pill, injection, sets this monstrous process into action with a guaranteed result of destruction unless active steps are taken to arrest it.

This brings us to the next key player—relapse. Relapse is best defined as a *process* that derails recovery. Relapse is a *process* rather than a single event because it often occurs so gradually that the affected individual is in trouble before they know it. Like currents in the ocean, relapse traps the unsuspecting victim, often with tragic results. Think of swimmers in the ocean, enjoying the sensation of gliding through the water. It all seems so innocent and safe. But if they forget to pay attention to their location in relation to the shore and are carried far out to sea, by the time they realize their dilemma, it may be too late.

Relapse creates a similar and equally deadly result. A person is in active relapse anytime shifts in feeling, thinking, or behavior draw them away from activities that promote a clean and sober life-style. It seems so safe and innocent as long as they don't drink or use. What does it matter where they go and whom they hang out with? What does it matter if they miss a meeting here and there or skip an antabuse tablet? The greatest danger of relapse is that it can but does not have to include the actual use of drugs or alcohol—at least not until its final stages! Unless the relapse process is identified and interrupted, a return to active substance abuse is as predictable as is the swimmer drowning.

When exploring the connection between anger and relapse, 10 key factors must be identified, understood, and counterbalanced to interrupt this destructive cycle. Only then will the potential for long-term, quality sobriety become possible.

1. Anger and relapse both generate involuntary physical reactions. These reactions (changes in heart rate, breathing, blood pressure, skin color, muscle tone, and so on) are not within our conscious control.
2. Anger and relapse both create shifts in how we feel emotionally.
3. Anger and relapse both create shifts in what we think.
4. Anger and relapse both influence how we decide to handle situations that occur on a daily basis in our lives.
5. Anger and relapse are both activated by specific triggers (people, places, things, thoughts, feelings).
6. Anger and relapse both produce warning signs (changes in body reactions, emotions, thoughts, behaviors) that signal the increasing risk of unproductive coping responses (poor anger management or active substance use).

7. Anger and relapse both produce an immediate sense of relief (I can avoid taking responsibility for life choices) that ultimately result in long-term negative consequences (conflicts in social, family, legal, and employment arenas; problems with health and/or mental health).
8. Anger and relapse each produce a cycle of self-destructive behavior that occurs more and more frequently unless interrupted and modified.
9. Anger and relapse are both influenced by past experiences, our worldview (what we believe is just and unjust), and the effectiveness of existing responses (if what I currently do has little negative consequence and gets me what I want, why would I change it?).
10. Anger and relapse create an explosive reaction (much like lighting a cigarette when oxygen is in use) that results in the worst possible outcome (the anger–relapse cycle continues to destroy its unsuspecting victim).

The final player in the anger–relapse cycle is *recovery*. Like relapse, recovery is a process that occurs over time. **Recovery does not mean you are cured!** It is a process of identifying factors that time after time lead you back to old patterns of destructive behavior. It means developing coping skills that help you combat risk factors and reassessing the effectiveness of these skills as life circumstances change. It also means using episodes of relapse as learning opportunities to help reduce your risk of repeating the same error next time. The ability to review feelings, thoughts, and behavior after a relapse allows you to strengthen your recovery plan. Recovery, to me, means having your life work more often than it doesn't and feel good more than it feels bad.

Recovery is the goal of the anger management/relapse prevention model presented in this book. It is not foolproof and requires a great deal of commitment and self-examination. One of my clients once asked me if I ever practice the things I teach in anger management. My response was "Yes, every day of my life." His second question was, "Does it work?" My response, "About 90% of the time. The other 10% of the time I still let my anger get the best of me. Although not an addict or alcoholic, I can self-destruct with the best of them by becoming verbally aggressive."

Because recovery is a process, you can't simply learn new skills and have life be smooth ever after. Real recovery requires you to apply, refine, modify, and practice coping skills on a regular basis. If you attend anger management classes and never practice what you learn there in the real world, or if you read this book and don't put the principles presented into action, you will continue to relapse with anger, addiction, or both. A wise person once said you teach that which you want to learn. I have been teaching clients to interrupt the anger–relapse cycle for 7 years. I still have a lot of learning to do and so do you!

2

Reactions and Responses

Most of us never question *why* we respond to situations in a certain way. Those who do question their motives generally believe it's "Just the way I am." This negative approach leaves us feeling powerless and trapped, doomed to carry out "set" patterns of behavior for the rest of our lives. The antidote for this dismal outlook involves challenging and expanding our existing knowledge base. Knowledge opens the door to self-discovery, therefore, we must understand that which we desire to change before successful intervention can occur. The following questions provide a starting point for this process:

1. What determines how we feel, think, and behave?
2. Are our patterns of response set in concrete or can they be changed?
3. How do we figure out what can and cannot be changed so the process of recovery can begin?

To answer these questions, we must expand the definitions of anger, addiction, and the anger–relapse cycle identified in chapter 1. An examination of the physical ingredients of anger is a good place to start. Think back to chapter 1 where we defined anger as a mixture of fear and pain. This combination triggers a survival reaction that is not within our conscious control. An example will help illustrate this concept: Picture a horse running in a pasture; a loud noise startles it and it accidentally runs into the barbed wire fence surrounding the pasture. The horse experiences fear because it is trapped and cannot free itself. It also experiences the physical pain of being repeatedly stuck by the barbs on the wire. This combination of fear and pain leads the horse to instinctively struggle to free itself. The more the horse struggles, the more damage is done. If someone comes along and tries to help the horse, because the animal cannot reason "this person is trying to help me," it will continue to react out of pain and fear, and the would-be helper can get kicked in the process.

Some of you may be thinking, "So what does that prove? Horses are dumb animals." Does this survival instinct also apply to humans? Let's look at another example. Picture a person caught in quicksand. He is fearful of being sucked under and is in pain from struggling against the weight of the quicksand as it covers his body. The more he struggles, the further he sinks into the quicksand. What if someone comes along and attempts to help? The trapped individual is so caught up in instinctive reactions, he will be unable to accept directions from the would-be rescuer. Efforts to have them grab a rope, stop struggling, reposition their body to keep their nose above the quicksand, are all ignored. If the rescuer attempts to grab the person he or she may be dragged into the quicksand and suffer a similar fate!

In both examples, the victims are unable to "think" about options. When instinct takes over, the organism, be it a mouse, horse, or human, automatically assumes a survival mode that, *while in progress*, cannot be interrupted. This is important information since one of our initial questions was, "How do we know what can and cannot be changed so the process of recovery can begin?" A brief review of the role our brain plays in creating emotional reactions will help us better understand this process.

The limbic system has been identified as the seat of all emotions. This part of the brain produces split-second decisions about whether an experience is potentially dangerous, painful, or pleasurable. Based on the examples provided above, both the horse and the human perceived their situations as dangerous and painful. This triggered a survival reaction (struggling to live). These instinct driven reactions are why soldiers can continue to fight in the presence of great fear and physical pain, why parents sacrifice themselves without thinking to save their young, and why firefighters, police officers, and others will place themselves at extreme risk of death or damage when attempting to rescue others.

We cannot alter instincts, so why mention them in this book? Again, it is equally important to know what we cannot change so we can focus energies on what *can* be changed. A second reason to explore instinct driven reactions is that we often *misperceive* incoming data and may activate our survival reactions unnecessarily. The goal, then, is to understand the basis for this misperception so we can develop more appropriate ways of managing our reactions (i.e., avoid activating our survival mode). An example will help you better understand this process.

Combat soldiers are frequently exposed to loud noises (rocket attacks, machine guns) that result in death or serious injury to those around them. They become hypersensitive to these sounds in order to survive. When they return to civilian life this hypersensitivity may be difficult to "turn off." They may hear a car backfire and assume an attack stance or dive to the ground. The survival skill that served them so well in combat now becomes a liability. Although we cannot alter this instinctive reaction, awareness of its origin and our probable reactions is useful information. Once awareness is gained, we can work to reduce the risk of overreacting. This will be discussed at length in chapter 4.

Three types of anger reactions are generated by the brain: predatory aggression, defensive aggression, and irritable aggression. Predatory aggression is the survival reaction we identified above. Again, it is based on a combination of fear and pain and our belief about what is happening. This type of anger reaction prepares the body to defend itself against possible sources of harm. It creates an immediate reaction— like pulling the lever on a breaker and turning lights on for a whole city block. If the threat does not quickly subside, the body "turns on" a second line of defense that makes us stronger, faster, and more powerful (this is why a one-hundred-pound woman can lift the front end of a car when her husband is trapped underneath). Again, these gut level reactions are not within conscious control. The sole purpose of this reaction is survival. As mentioned earlier, this type of anger reaction is not subject to conscious efforts of change. We can, however, learn to identify patterns of overreaction and this will be explored further in upcoming chapters.

The second type of anger reaction is defensive aggression. This type of reaction is also geared toward self-preservation; however, unlike predatory aggression, it involves conscious thought. In instances involving defensive aggression the individual has a brief period of time to think before selecting a response. An example will help demonstrate the difference between these types of anger reactions. You are on your way home late one night and realize you need some cash for the following morning. You stop at an unfamiliar ATM to get the money so you won't be pressed for time the next day. As you approach the machine, you see two individuals loitering nearby. If you reacted with predatory aggression, you would instinctively attack them to counteract their potential to harm you. A defensive–aggressive reaction would involve thought. You would certainly become uncomfortable and aware of the potential need to fight or flee. Based on this awareness you have several response choices. You can take the risk of getting the money while keeping an eye on the loiterers, and hope that nothing happens. In this case, you would be prepared to fight if necessary and would remain on guard until safely in your car and moving down the road. Another choice would be to abort the transaction and seek another, safer location to complete your business. Similar to predatory aggression, you are alert and sensing danger. Unlike predatory aggression, you consciously weigh your choices and act accordingly. Since defensive and predatory aggressive reactions are primarily designed for survival, they are not the focus of the anger management/relapse prevention program. However, as with predatory aggression, we sometimes overreact and become defensive when it is unnecessary. Therefore, the goal is to more accurately assess our beliefs about what is happening so more appropriate response choices can be selected.

The final type of anger reaction, irritable aggression, is the primary focus of this book. Irritable aggression involves the day-to-day frustrations that drive us to acts of desperation. They are the glasses of spilled milk, the car that cuts us off on the freeway, the missed appointments, unexpected weekend guests, canceled vacations, and so forth. These events generate changes in body reactions, and in how we feel, think, and behave. They also greatly influence our relapse potential (i.e., "It was a terrible week, I deserve a drink!"; "You would have run that guy off the road too if you were me!"; "How else do you expect me to keep my sanity, one little joint won't hurt!"; "If you had to live with *my* husband/wife, you'd drink, drug, have temper tantrums, withdraw . . . too!").

Irritable aggression is a less potent (but equally dangerous) form of anger that signals displeasure with someone or something. Its more subtle qualities often lead us to discount the tremendous impact it has in our lives. Irritable aggression is frequently ignored or pushed back out of our awareness so we can deal with "more important things." This tendency to delay coping with small problems gives them time to grow into big problems. The good news: Irritable aggression is *highly* responsive to change! This means we can learn to recognize and defuse irritable aggression and avoid selecting response choices that trigger relapse or other negative consequences in our lives. This book will teach you to recognize factors that trigger irritable aggression and introduces a number of strategies designed to counteract its negative impact on your life.

Irritable aggression makes up half of the anger–relapse cycle. The fragile physical and emotional state of a person in early recovery creates a situation much like mixing sleeping pills and alcohol. Each is potentially dangerous but when mixed together, look out! Individuals in early recovery are struggling to regain physical and emotional balance (the body worked hard to create a sense of balance during active addiction and must now work equally hard to adjust to its new chemical-free state). This adjustment process increases the risk for irritable aggression (things that would not normally bother a person make them want to pull out their hair)! Therefore, early sobriety plus a lowered tolerance for stress significantly increases relapse potential. Chapters 5 through 13 offer a variety of coping skills to interrupt this process.

Because the anger–relapse cycle is affected by emotional and social as well as physical factors, our focus now shifts to three additional ingredients influencing this process: What we have learned from life experiences, our beliefs about what is happening to and around us, and whether or not our current behavior gets us what we want and need. Let's begin by exploring *learned behavior*. This phrase, simply stated, means what you came to know about defining the people, places, and things in your life. An example is the story of how to prepare a ham. A young woman noticed that at each family dinner her mother always cut both ends of the ham off before cooking it. She could not identify any reason for this behavior, so one day asked her mother, "Mama, why do you always cut the ends off the ham before cooking it?" The mother looked at her daughter and responded, "Well, I never really thought about it. My mother always did it, so I thought it was what I should do." The young woman still curious as to how this custom got started went to her grandmother. She asked, "Grandma, why do you always cut the ends off the ham before cooking it?" The grandmother laughed and replied, "Well honey, in my day the ovens were small and we had to cut the ends off the ham so it would fit in the oven." This is a classic example of a learned behavior that was passed innocently from generation to generation even after its purpose was forgotten and no longer necessary. We will explore the influence of learned behavior on the anger–relapse cycle in chapter 3.

A second ingredient involves how we explain what is happening to and around us. Our beliefs play a major role in the choices we make in daily life. Past experiences and their outcomes shape our beliefs, thus our responses, as we approach new experiences. For example, if a large dog bites me when I am 3 years old I may develop a fear of large dogs. My fear is not so much based on the presence of a large dog as it is on my belief (based on my childhood experience of having been bitten) that *all* large dogs are dangerous. This idea will be discussed at length in chapter 4.

Finally, the effectiveness of existing responses greatly influences our degree of motivation for change. If I drink and drive and my parents keep bailing me out of jail and paying my fines, why would I be motivated to change? If I can threaten, yell, and bully others into doing things my way, why would I want to learn how to become less aggressive? If I spend the rent money every month on alcohol and drugs and my significant other always covers the bills, what motivation do I have to change? If, on the other hand, my driving while intoxicated charges land me in jail or prison with stiff fines and license revocation, I may decide it is time to change my ways. If I yell, scream, and bully others and find myself divorced and unemployed, I may want to rethink how I interact with others. If my significant other refuses to cover expenses and makes arrangements to stay elsewhere until I agree to become more responsible, I may become motivated to change so I can avoid further losses. In short, if my current behavior costs more than it gives me, I will have greater motivation to change. If it gives me more than it costs, my motivation for change will be poor. This concept will also receive further attention in subsequent chapters.

A final goal of this chapter is to identify the relationship between anger and addiction that sustains the relapse cycle. Relapse and recovery are processes that require ongoing observation. This means we must continuously monitor thoughts, feelings, and behavior for shifts signaling increasing risk of relapse. A variety of coping skills are needed to maintain recovery and these too require careful monitoring so they can be modified, updated, or replaced when no longer effective. When we lack awareness of our current feelings, thoughts, and behaviors, and the role these factors play in the relapse process, and either do not possess or fail to apply coping skills to redirect anger, the potential for returning to former patterns of self-defeating response choices is high. On the contrary, once we learn to recognize faulty patterns of feeling, thinking, and behaving, and develop and apply adequate coping skills, our relapse potential is greatly reduced (refer to models 1 and 2).

Model 1: High Relapse Potential

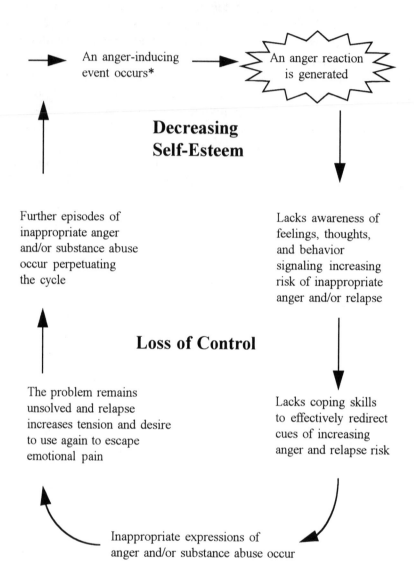

An anger-inducing event occurs*

An anger reaction is generated

Decreasing Self-Esteem

Further episodes of inappropriate anger and/or substance abuse occur perpetuating the cycle

Lacks awareness of feelings, thoughts, and behavior signaling increasing risk of inappropriate anger and/or relapse

Loss of Control

The problem remains unsolved and relapse increases tension and desire to use again to escape emotional pain

Lacks coping skills to effectively redirect cues of increasing anger and relapse risk

Inappropriate expressions of anger and/or substance abuse occur

* The individual is trapped in a self-fulfilling cycle of negative responses and believes there is no escape.

From *Anger and addiction: Breaking the relapse cycle*, by J. Clancy, 1996. Madison, CT: Psychosocial Press. Adapted with publisher's permission.

Model 2: Low Relapse Potential

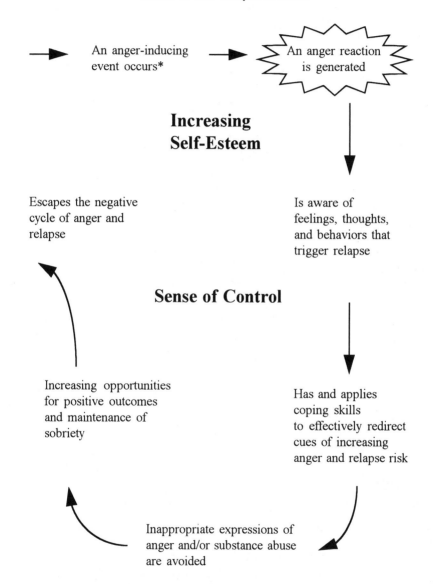

An anger-inducing event occurs*

An anger reaction is generated

Increasing Self-Esteem

Escapes the negative cycle of anger and relapse

Is aware of feelings, thoughts, and behaviors that trigger relapse

Sense of Control

Increasing opportunities for positive outcomes and maintenance of sobriety

Has and applies coping skills to effectively redirect cues of increasing anger and relapse risk

Inappropriate expressions of anger and/or substance abuse are avoided

* The individual identifies strategies to change self-destructive feelings, thoughts, and behaviors and selects response choices that allow them to escape the anger–relapse cycle.

From *Anger and addiction: Breaking the relapse cycle*, by J. Clancy, 1996. Madison, CT: Psychosocial Press. Adapted with publisher's permission.

3

The Patches on Your Quilt

When my oldest son was born his great-grandmother made a beautiful quilt to commemorate his birth. This quilt contained several hundred patches carefully woven together to tell his family story. Each patch had a family member's name and a picture telling something about the individual's character. During the quilting process, my son's great-grandmother would show me a patch and tell me its meaning. As the quilt took form, the family's history began to unfold. When the quilt was finally finished, we held it up to view the results. It provided a moving account of the circumstances each generation of the family had endured across time. As I looked at the quilt it suddenly dawned on me that I was seeing the life of a family unfold. This quilt represented individual members, and the events of their lives, that when woven together produced a legacy of beliefs and behaviors to be passed from generation to generation.

The significance of this story becomes clear when we look at the quilt first in pieces and then as a whole. If individual pieces are observed separately rather than as parts of a whole, we see only fragments. We may develop insights about specific family members but we never appreciate the family as a whole. These individual patches, although important, represent separate chapters in the family's life. Like a book with

21

missing pages, the disconnected patches leave the viewer feeling confused and frustrated. To bring a family's history to life we must view the quilt as a whole. Only then can we appreciate this family's strengths and weaknesses, its struggles and triumphs, why individual members loved and hated certain things, pursued certain dreams and not others, and so forth.

By now you are probably wondering how this story fits in a book about anger and relapse. The relevance of this story is that our behavior is not created in a vacuum. The way we feel, think, and behave is gradually shaped by family interactions and expanded through a series of life experiences. Like the patches of a quilt, if individual events are viewed separately, they have little meaning. If, however, these events are woven together, we begin to appreciate why we feel, think, and behave as we do. This chapter begins the process of identifying the patches of your quilt, the legacy of your childhood experiences that so subtly shaped and continue to influence your response choices.

The most difficult part of designing a quilt is deciding where to begin. What patches can best illustrate the story as it unfolds? In what order should these patches be attached to the main quilt? A review of childhood experiences should be one of the first patches you sew on your quilt. Unless you understand what drives your current behavior, coping skills introduced in later chapters will not achieve their full potential. We are often cautioned by well-meaning family and friends to "leave the past behind and move on." Although we cannot alter the past, a carefully guided review of past experiences can be useful as we attempt to understand how and why we came to be who we are. Much like the foundation of a house, this first patch on your quilt, the threads representing the experiences in your life, provide a foundation for recovery.

The exercise described in this chapter, if completed with truth and sincerity, will be one of the most difficult you encounter. It requires you to look backward in time and examine experiences that occurred during periods of your life when you were the most vulnerable. The purpose is *not* to blame and shame others or make excuses for your own behavior. I genuinely believe there are no bad people just people displaying destructive behavior. Even the most unspeakable acts can be defined as acts of desperation carried out by people with little understanding of why they behave as they do and even less understanding of how they might conduct themselves differently. This statement does not excuse destructive behavior, it simply provides a frame of reference from which it can be objectively viewed. Think about it for a moment. How many people would deliberately place themselves in positions of being abused or abusing others if they really thought other choices existed?

To that end, all childhood experiences, from the most nurturing and loving to the most abusive and destructive, shape and continue to influence our worldview and our particular style of interacting with others. People rarely view past experiences unless they are "blaming the victim" or "blaming the world." I invite you to shift your focus from blaming and assigning blame to seeking understanding. The goal of this chapter is to teach you how to strategically place this patch on your quilt so it becomes a catalyst for change rather than an excuse to continue current patterns of unproductive behavior.

As you review past experiences, remember that most of the messages we receive in childhood are nonverbal. This means we learn more from watching others than from listening to what they say. Ideally families would sit down with their children and say, "Well children, tonight we are going to teach you how to appropriately share your feelings. We will demonstrate the proper way to express fear, anger, joy, and sadness. We will also identify healthy ways to cope with life experiences when you feel confused or hopeless." If learning was that straightforward, people would be much better prepared to establish and maintain relationships with family members, friends, coworkers, and intimate partners.

In reality, most of the messages we receive in childhood come through nonverbal cues. We watch what others say and do and model our behavior accordingly. In some families, yelling and throwing things is considered normal by the participants. In other families, this type of behavior would be viewed as abusive. To further complicate the learning process, messages we receive from others may be confusing. Our parents and other important role models often say one thing and do another. A classic example is when the parent spanks Johnny while saying, "Johnny, I told you not to hit your sister! Hitting is bad behavior!" This mixed message leaves the child confused (i.e., is hitting good or bad? My parent said hitting is bad but then they hit me! How do I know if hitting is good or bad since I heard one thing and experienced another?). These messages are processed unconsciously and called into play when experiences in our lives activate memories of these past events.

Finally, we cannot ever completely erase the messages we receive in childhood. The old saying "sticks and stones can break my bones but words can never harm me" is a myth! Think back in your own childhood. The skinned knees, cuts, and scratches all healed and were forgotten. The hurtful statements made by family members, classmates, teachers, and others in our lives formed scars that we carry for the rest of our lives. The good news is once we identify the source and meaning of these damaging messages, they can be challenged and altered. The memory remains but we can develop a skill for remembering and letting go—placing the painful message in perspective so it loses its power to drive us to acts of destruction and despair. Two examples from my own childhood will help illustrate this process in action.

As a child, I remember my family being very happy and peaceful. My parents never fought or openly disagreed. My picture of a happy family was one in which all members always get along. I remember one incident where my father and oldest sister had a verbal disagreement. This incident, although certainly not abusive, so frightened my middle sister and I that we collapsed to the floor in a flood of tears. It was beyond our understanding that family members could and did disagree at times. The unspoken message that loving families never disagree shaped our beliefs about love and marriage. The result, an idealistic view that could not possibly sustain itself in the real world. Not surprising, all three of our first marriages ended in divorce.

During my process of self-discovery I asked my mother why she and my father never fought or disagreed. She explained that both she and my father came from homes where conflict was frequent and destructive. Before they married they vowed never to create such an atmosphere for their own children. Their intention was to shield us from the harsh reality that relationships sometimes go terribly wrong in spite of the partners' best efforts. Their unwitting mistake was to present a one-sided view of relationships. We never learned that conflict in relationships is not only normal but necessary. That conflict, if productively handled, can actually strengthen and enrich the bond between partners and friends.

Were my parents wrong? Did they scar my sisters and I for life? The answer is no! The patches on their quilts (memories of emotionally painful childhood experiences) shaped their behavior as partners and parents. They taught us what they thought would help us be happy children and well-adjusted adults. Reviewing this patch on my quilt, although painful, helped me develop a great appreciation of how hard it is to be a partner and a parent. It also allowed me to examine, challenge, and modify beliefs that once exposed, were no longer valid.

A second childhood event that greatly influenced my view of relationships and the world was the sudden, unexpected death of my father when he was 44. I had recently purchased a horse and he spent that Saturday morning repairing her stall so she would have safe housing. On his way home, he suffered a massive heart attack. Quite by accident, I decided to ride my horse home that day. I found my father lying on the porch swing fatally wounded. He gently asked me to get help, and fast. I was only 12 and panicked. I did not have my house key so ran frantically from window to window calling out for my mother and sisters to open the door. My child's mind could not realize that no one was home or that I should seek a neighbor's help. My father, with great effort, struggled to his feet. I supported him as we walked to a neighbor's house for help. The last memory I have of that terrible day is my father's face, filled with pain and fear, and my sense of terror and inadequacy—the belief that I had made a horrible, irrevocable mistake. His death two days later reinforced this belief; that my inadequate response had caused this event that would forever change my family.

After my father's death I was filled with an unspeakable anger. I proceeded to spew defensive, hostile reactions onto everyone and everything in my path. I also became a superachiever, always striving to do myself one better no matter what the cost. Reviewing this event as an adult I discovered my anger had been a reaction to the overwhelming fear and grief that resulted from my father's death. My desire to superachieve stemmed from a desperate need to "prove" to myself that I really was a capable human being. These unspoken messages were based on faulty beliefs that I had never dared to challenge. As I reviewed this patch on my quilt, I realized that I could not have changed the outcome of this event no matter what I had done—the damage to my father's heart was too great. I also realized I could not undo the years of anger and overachievement that followed this event. I finally began to understand why I was such an angry, driven person. Conscious awareness of this process allowed me to challenge my beliefs about this terrible event. Only then could I begin to develop and apply coping skills to interrupt the cycle of anger and overachievement. Although still far from perfect,

I now redirect my anger constructively more often than not and can consciously choose whether to risk participating in activities that send me into overdrive.

Having set the stage, I now invite you to explore the patches on your own family quilt (see Worksheet 1). The goal is to develop greater awareness and appreciation of how you came to be the person that you are. Be honest with yourself and remember, this exercise is not about blaming and shaming, it is about learning and growing. It is the first step in learning to interrupt the anger–relapse cycle.

WORKSHEET 1

Reviewing the Patches on Your Quilt

This worksheet is designed to assist you in exploring how role models and past experiences shaped and continue to influence your feelings, thoughts, and behavior. Although this exercise may uncover painful memories, the cleansing effect of releasing this material provides a foundation for recovery.

1. Who was your primary role model during childhood? _____

2. How did this person express anger? _____

3. Did this person use drugs or alcohol to cope with feelings?   YES _____   NO _____

4. What "messages" did you receive about expressing your feelings and needs? _____

5. Were verbal and nonverbal messages consistent or contradictory? _____

6. How did you feel as a child when you received messages from this person? _____

Worksheet 1 (continued)

7. How do you feel as an adult when you look back on these messages and how they influenced your life?

_____

8. What similarities and differences do you see in yourself and this person in the way feelings and needs are expressed? _____

9. If you had the power to "change" the messages that guide your life choices, how would you rewrite them?

Old Message: _____

New Message: _____

Old Message: _____

New Message: _____

Old Message: _____

New Message: _____

10. Do you believe you *can* change your thoughts and behavior? YES _____ NO _____

If NO, what would it take for you to believe that change is possible? _____

11. What action can you take to initiate this process? _____

_____

Adapted with the publisher's permission from: *Learning to live without violence: A handbook for men*, by Daniel J. Sonkin and Michael Durphy, 1982. Volcano, CA: Volcano Press.

4

Kerosene and Campfires

When I was a little girl my family went camping every summer at a local state park. My mother was usually in charge of starting the campfire. This was a fascinating process that I watched with great anticipation— I knew that the campfire meant hot dogs and marshmallows! My mother carefully cleaned out the fire pit and laid tiny bits of tinder to serve as a foundation for the fire. She then laid her kindling, small sticks that fed the fire once the tinder was consumed. Next came the logs. These were carefully placed at 90-degree angles over the tinder and kindling. Once she was satisfied with the arrangement of logs, old newspaper was placed strategically between the logs to encourage the fire to burn. Finally, a match was lit and applied to the paper in several locations. The budding fire was carefully fanned until my mother felt sure it was hot enough to burn on its own. This process of starting a fire was a carefully orchestrated event. Each step building on the one before, leading us closer and closer to our evening campfire.

My husband is from New York and only began camping about 12 years ago. Our first camping trip showed how different North and South can be! The first night we began building a campfire, I collected tinder and kindling intending to build our fire with the same precision my mother had always demonstrated. My husband, with a look of exasperation, stated,

"If you go through all those steps, it will be morning before we have a fire! Let me show you a faster way." He proceeded to toss wood into the fire pit until it was full. He doused the entire structure with kerosene, backed up, lit a match, and threw it in. The fire ignited with a flash of light and a loud boom. I was appalled by this display of campfire chemistry! The look on my face must have shown my surprise. My husband calmly said, "It may be dramatic but the results sure are quicker!"

When I tell this story, most of my clients liken their episodes of anger and relapse to the way my husband ignites a fire. "Gee Jo, my anger comes up so suddenly I have no warning!" Or, "I'm humming along minding my own business and then wham I relapse!" Unless you are brain damaged or inebriated this is rarely the case. There is always a buildup process. Sometimes it is quick and visible, sometimes slow and discrete, but this process is always in action! Anger and relapse are much like the construction of a carefully planned campfire. Changes in feelings, thoughts, and behavior often occur days or even weeks before we experience a relapse with anger or substances. This chapter teaches you to recognize triggers and cues that serve as warning signs of increasing anger or relapse potential. Once identified, you can monitor your buildup process and customize coping skills to redirect anger and reduce the potential for relapse.

I know, you still don't believe me! I can hear you thinking "Well she just doesn't understand that I am different. My reactions happen so fast I don't have time to recognize and redirect them!" Let's look at another example to challenge your skepticism. Picture a sleek, new, red, Ferrari in your driveway. It's fast, it's classy, it can go from zero to 60 in 5.2 seconds! Now, let's look closer. Even a sleek, shiny, new sports car goes through a buildup process before it can do the zero to 60 number. First, a person has to put a key in the ignition. Then, the ignition must be engaged by turning the key. The driver has to step on the clutch, engage the gears, and step on the gas to activate the car. It may go zero to 60 in 5.2 but if you don't go through these steps, it won't do zero to 60 at all!

A second example is a box of dynamite with different lengths of fuses. One section has sticks with 1-inch fuses, another section has sticks with 12-inch fuses, and the third section has sticks with fuses 50 feet long. If I am the person handling the dynamite, and I have to run 50 yards to reach safety before the dynamite explodes, I doubt I would choose sticks from the section with 1-inch fuses! Well folks, people are like sticks of dynamite. Some of us have short fuses, some have medium fuses, and some have fuses so long we think they're brain dead! The first step in learning to recognize your buildup process is to identify the length of your fuse. What I know about myself is that I am much like a racehorse pacing nervously at the starting gate. Inevitably I am the horse that breaks the wire before the bell rings! Knowing that I have a short fuse alerts me to pay very close attention to my triggers and cues so coping skills can be applied immediately once my buildup process is activated. This skill takes time to develop and the exercises presented in this chapter serve as a starting point.

We can begin this process by defining exactly what is meant by the terms *triggers* and *cues*. Cues are the warning signs that anger and relapse potential are increasing. There are four categories of cues:

1. *Physical cues* are changes that occur in our bodies signaling a need to prepare for fighting or fleeing. Examples include increased heart rate, rapid breathing, muscle tension, stomach cramps, aches and pains in areas where we have old scars or wounds, hair standing up on your neck or other parts of your body, flushing red or turning pale, sweating, having your pupils dilate or contract, and so on. These cues are *involuntary* which means we do not call them into play, they happen automatically. Although we cannot control their occurrence, we can learn to identify them as they appear.

Another interesting fact about physical cues is that if you pay close attention, you will discover they occur in a specific order. I may first experience a racing heart, followed by muscle tension, and then flushing. This order or hierarchy of symptom presentation is extremely important, especially if I have a short fuse. If I can recognize that my buildup process has been activated when I notice my heart racing, I can *immediately* apply a coping skill to interrupt this process. If I wait until I flush, I may be so out of control that I misdirect my anger and/or relapse.

2. *Emotional cues* are changes in our mood that occur when we encounter certain experiences. Emotional cues involve five basic feelings: happy, sad, scared, confused, and angry. These cues, if identified, alert us to pay close attention to how we are thinking and acting, since mood, mind, and matter are intricately linked and determine how we ultimately choose to respond.

3. *Cognitive cues* involve our thoughts. Just what do we tell our-selves about what we are feeling and experiencing at given points in time? Since thoughts can be either positive or negative, they greatly influence how we feel and behave. This will be discussed at length in a later chapter.

4. *Behavioral cues* are what we do with our feelings and thoughts. These cues include pacing, cursing, hitting, yelling, withdrawing, get-ting quiet, wiggling, clenching your fists, wrinkling your brow, twirl-ing your hair, picking at your clothes, making or avoiding eye contact, and so forth. Behavioral cues are the final link in a chain reaction that begins with physical cues and ends with a behavior.

When we view physical, emotional, cognitive, and behavioral cues separately, they make little sense. Like the patches on a quilt, we must carefully piece them together and view the finished product to achieve maximum appreciation of their combined effect. Again, the order in which these cues appear is critical to successful application of all the coping skills that will be introduced in this book. An example might better illustrate this point. When I make peanut brittle a candy thermometer is essential so I will know when the candy is done. The mercury in the thermometer gradually rises as the temperature of the candy increases. I must carefully monitor this process in order to create peanut brittle with the right texture. If I remove it from the stove before it reaches a certain temperature, it will be soft and runny. If I allow the temperature to get too high, it will burn and be tough. Once the mistake is made, I cannot recook or uncook the candy. I have to start over again with fresh ingre-dients and will one hopes have learned a lesson that will help prevent similar outcomes in the future. The anger–relapse cycle follows a simi-lar course. If we recognize cues of increasing anger and relapse before they reach the critical point of no return, coping skills can be applied to redirect the outcome. Once the process has gone too far, we cannot in-terrupt it. What we can do is use the incident as a learning experience reducing the risk of a repeat performance (see model 3).

Now that we understand what cues are and how they activate the anger–relapse cycle, the next step is defining the term *triggers*. A trigger is a person, place, or thing that activates some or all of the cue catego-ries identified above. Triggers can also be thought of in terms of who, what, why, when, and where. Let's take a closer look at these terms.

Model 3: The Continuum of Anger and Relapse

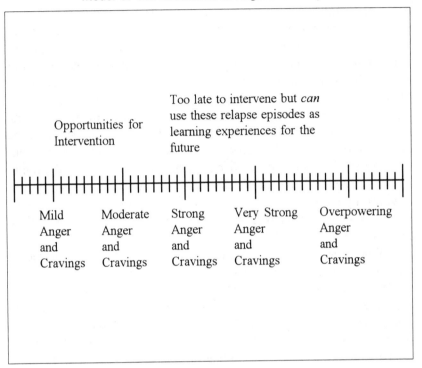

Opportunities for Intervention

Too late to intervene but *can* use these relapse episodes as learning experiences for the future

| Mild Anger and Cravings | Moderate Anger and Cravings | Strong Anger and Cravings | Very Strong Anger and Cravings | Overpowering Anger and Cravings |

1. How we are related to an individual (friend, family, coworker, stranger, and so on), and the state of our relationship with this person (close, estranged, conflicted, indifferent, no established relationship at all), plays a critical role in the activation of cues. For instance, if I wear a red dress and my husband says, "Jo, you really look awful in red," I can have several reactions. If our relationship is good, I might say, "Thanks for telling me, I'll choose another color." If our relationship is in conflict this might be just the ammunition I need to launch a counter-attack! The same comment from a stranger might have little or no impact at all since I have no relationship with them and really don't care what they think about my red dress.

2. *What* refers to the actions and comments others initiate or withhold, and *why* targets our thinking about their motives for either taking action or remaining passive. Again, our relationship to the person influences our beliefs about what their action or inaction means. Let's look at an example. I am on the checkout line at the grocery store. I hear a commotion and look to see where all the noise is coming from. I see a woman with four small children and a heavily laden shopping cart coming around the corner. She heads toward the checkout counter and pushes her cart in front of mine. My response will be greatly influenced by our relationship and what I think about her intentions. Since she's a stranger, obviously, we have no relationship so I have no reason to extend special favors to her. Since I have children, I may be empathetic and think to myself, "I bet she was so preoccupied with all those children that she didn't even see my basket in front of her." With this belief, I would probably say nothing and allow her to cut the line. On the other hand, I might think to myself, "How rude! I don't know who she thinks she is, it's obvious my basket was in front of her." With this belief, I would most likely challenge her behavior and demand that she take her proper place in the line.

Words and phrases can also trigger a variety of responses based on what we think about specific comments and why we think they were made. Take the phrase, "I am from Pasadena, Texas." Depending on what my experience with people from Pasadena has been, I may have very different reactions. When I teach classes on triggers and cues I often use this phrase to see what reactions surface. During one class, a Caucasian man indicated that he was from Texas and had once dated a cowgirl from Pasadena. This phrase reminded him of his former girl friend and the good times they had shared at local rodeos and clubs. Another client, a black man, had a strong negative reaction. When asked to identify his source of his reaction he stated: "Pasadena, Texas, is Ku Klux Klan country. My grandfather was badly beaten by the Klan and I hate all those bigots from Pasadena." This is an excellent example of how past experiences influence what becomes a trigger in our lives. In each case, it was not so much *what* was said that determined each client's response, it was the *meaning* attached to the words. Pay close attention to your interpretations of what others say and do, and also to what they fail to say and do. Sometimes what is *not* said and done creates triggers as powerful as what *is* said and done! A final example will illustrate this point.

You have arranged to meet a friend at a local restaurant for dinner. This person is someone you really like but have only known a short time. You hope to build a solid friendship and this dinner is an important part of the process. You arrive at the restaurant and after 30 minutes ask the waiter if your party has come in or called and receive a negative response. You wait another 30 minutes and finally order dinner and eat alone. When you arrive home, you call your friend, and leave a hot message on the answering machine. When they call to discuss it, you hang up, and resolve never to speak to them again. This response is based on *what* you thought about *why* your friend missed dinner. There may have been a very good explanation but your interpretation prevented you from even considering this possibility (chapter 6 will address this process in great detail).

3. The moment *when* something occurs also determines whether or not it becomes a trigger. I took two semesters of economics in college. I worked very hard in both courses but made C's each time. Luckily, I was at the end of my sophomore year and had a track record of straight A's. I decided that economics was just not my subject and let it go at that. If I had received these C's early in my college career, it might have negatively influenced my future performance. Pay attention to *when* things happen in your life. During childhood and other times of vulnerability, events such as the one described above can greatly influence what does or doesn't become an anger or relapse trigger.

4. *Where* we are when certain events unfold also plays a role in whether or not the event becomes a trigger. Say you work in a large typing pool and your workstation is in a room with many other workers. Your boss, dissatisfied with some piece of your work, proceeds to correct you in front of your coworkers. This is both embarrassing and humiliating. You have to correct the piece of work in question, but more importantly, you must face and live down comments from your coworkers. If, on the other hand, your boss reviews the problems with your work privately, the event, although unpleasant, is much less distressing. The *consequences* of an event, based on the setting in which it occurs, activates or defuses potential triggers.

The first step in learning to redirect anger and reduce relapse potential involves identifying your *personal pattern of triggers and cues*. What people, places, and things act as triggers in your life? What cues alert you that a trigger has activated your buildup process, and in what order do these cues appear? Most of you are clueless when I ask these questions. You can tell me how you ultimately handle situations but not what activated the buildup process or what cues pointed to impending episodes of misdirected anger or relapse. The anger management/relapse prevention journal (see Worksheet 2, pp. 38–41) is designed to help you begin the process of recognizing your personal pattern of triggers and cues. Early identification is vital to successful application of coping skills introduced in chapters 5 through 13 in this book.

Successful use of the journal requires commitment. Many people make excuses about why they can't complete journal entries. The biggest rationalization I hear time and time again is, "Gee Jo, I'm just too busy to keep a journal." Effective journal keeping only takes 5 or 10 minutes a day. The key is making entries *every day*. If you put it off and try to catch up at the end of a week, you will become frustrated and give up.

Successful journal keeping also requires honesty. This means you must evaluate your performance in a variety of situations and decide whether you really handled it as well as possible. Honest evaluation of your actions and their consequences is *not* about punishing yourself for poor response choices! It involves a careful review of your buildup process so coping skills to redirect the outcome of an event can be applied in a more timely fashion. The anger–relapse cycle is much like tumblers on a safe. All three numbers must line up or the safe will not open. The anger–relapse cycle can only occur when triggers and cues are allowed to "line up." This journal, if used correctly, will keep your tumblers tumbling so the factors leading to relapse have less opportunities to line up.

When making journal entries avoid discounting "little angers" and "tiny cravings!" Anger and relapse exist on a continuum which goes from mild to extreme. We easily recognize rage and overpowering urges to drink or use drugs. What we often fail to notice are the mild irritations and subtle cravings that occur in everyday life. These "little angers" and "tiny cravings" are probably the biggest factor in the anger–relapse cycle. When enough of these angers and cravings accumulate, we relapse, misdirect our anger, or both. Tracking patterns of response across time, both to mild and extreme angers and cravings, increases our potential to interrupt the anger–relapse cycle.

Finally, see journal keeping as an ongoing process. Just when you think you are an expert at recognizing triggers and cues, life circumstances will create shifts in your response style. Age, illness, stressful events, and change in general create shifts in physical reactions, feelings, thoughts, and yes, behaviors. Keeping an anger management/relapse prevention journal is a bit like keeping a garden. If you weed and feed it regularly you will always have fresh vegetables and daily maintenance will require minimal effort. If, however, you let nature take its course, your garden will become full of weeds and it will take great effort to regain control. How will you decide to keep your garden?

WORKSHEET 2

THE ANGER MANAGEMENT/RELAPSE PREVENTION JOURNAL

The anger management/relapse prevention journal is designed to help you track patterns of feeling, thinking, and behavior across time. Daily entries are suggested to get the most benefit from your journal. Use the attached worksheets to document triggers and cues when you feel yourself becoming angry or at risk for relapse. Include the following information:

1. Day of the week, time of day, and date. This is important because it pinpoints times that may be especially difficult for you, and therefore place you at greater risk for misdirected anger and relapse.

2. What physical, emotional, cognitive, and behavioral cues alerted you that anger or relapse risks were increasing? Remember this relates to what you *feel* inside, your *emotional state*, your *thoughts*, and how you *behave*. Also remember to note the order in which these cues appear.

3. Describe the situation that occurred *immediately* before you felt your anger or relapse risks increasing. Remember to include the following:

   a. Whom were you with? _____

   b. Where were you? _____

   c. What were you doing? _____

4. How intense was your anger reaction or urge to use substances?

Mild _____ Moderate _____ Strong _____ Very Strong _____ Overpowering _____

5. What steps did you take to cope with your anger or urges to use substances?

6. Were you satisfied with your response?   YES _____   NO _____

7. If you answered NO to question 6, what would you do differently next time you face a similar situation?

8. Remember to use your journal on a regular basis. Bedtime is a good time to take a few minutes to fill out your worksheets. Buy a spiral notebook and use the sample worksheet in this book to set up your anger management/relapse prevention journal.

9. *At least once a week review your journal entries.* The goal is to identify *patterns* of reactions, feelings, thoughts, and behavior that increase your risk of misdirected anger and relapse. Pay special attention to the time of day, day of the week, and time of the year. With time and faithful journal keeping you will learn to recognize times that require greater effort to navigate without having an episode of misdirected anger or a relapse. Also pay close attention to where you are, whom you are with, and what you are doing from entry to entry. Is there a pattern that influences your risk for misdirected anger or relapse? If so, develop a plan to modify your exposure to these factors, or if not possible, plan ahead so coping skills can be applied at the earliest possible moment.

GOOD LUCK!

Adapted with the publisher's permission from: *Learning to live without violence: A handbook for men*, by Daniel J. Sonkin and Michael Durphy, 1982. Volcano, CA: Volcano Press.

Worksheet 2 (continued)

THE ANGER MANAGEMENT/RELAPSE PREVENTION JOURNAL
DAILY WORKSHEET

Date: _____   Time of Day: _____   Day of the Week: _____

Signs of Increasing Anger or Relapse

Physical Signs

Emotional Signs

Changes in Thinking

Behavioral Signs

1. Describe the situation that occurred *immediately* before you noticed your anger or relapse potential increasing (whom were you with, where were you, what were you doing?): _____

    _____

    _____

2. How intense was your anger reaction or urge to use substances?

    Mild _____ Moderate _____ Strong _____ Very Strong _____ Overpowering _____

3. What steps did you take to cope with your anger or urge to use? _____

    _____

4. Were you satisfied with your response? YES _____ NO _____

5. If NO, what will you do differently next time you face a similar situation? _____

    _____

Adapted with the publisher's permission from: *Learning to live without violence: A handbook for men*, by Daniel J. Sonkin and Michael Durphy, 1982. Volcano, CA: Volcano Press.

5

Turning Down Your Thermostat

Imagine a thermostat like the one used to adjust the temperature in your house. It has a dial you can turn to give the furnace and air conditioner commands about how hot or cool to keep your home. When a thermostat is working correctly, it keeps your home at a pleasant temperature and saves both energy and money. Unfortunately, thermostats sometimes fail. The outcome is generally not serious; you call a repairman or replace the thermostat. Occasionally, the outcome is not so pleasant, as was the case when my family went out of town for the weekend one summer. We set our thermostat on 78 degrees to conserve energy and set out extra food and water for our pet gerbil. Satisfied that all was in order, we went merrily on our way. When we returned home Sunday night and opened the door, we knew immediately that something was terribly wrong. The house felt like a furnace and the thermostat read 105 degrees. I immediately ran to the gerbil cage and the poor little creature was in the throes of death from heat exhaustion and dehydration. It was a very upsetting experience to say the least!

Our response choices are a lot like thermostats. When we are feeling well and have enough coping skills, we can easily control how we respond in given situations. We consider what is taking place around us and act accordingly. Unfortunately, just as thermostats in houses break down, our ability to manage feelings, thoughts, and behavior can break down during periods of prolonged stress, exhaustion, or confusion. This is especially true if we lack coping skills to relieve our distress. This chapter introduces the time-out technique, one of nine strategies identified in this book, to help you reset your thermostat when things go awry. It marks the beginning of part 2 in the recovery process: identifying and learning to apply coping skills to counteract triggers and cues identified in chapters 1 through 4.

Time-out is often defined as a form of punishment. "Okay, Johnny, you were a bad boy so go put your nose in the corner for 10 minutes," or "Susie, go sit in your time-out chair for 5 minutes. I bet next time I tell you to stop banging those pots you'll remember!" From my viewpoint, it is simply an opportunity to back up and regroup *before* you select a response choice. This technique creates a safety valve, much like that of a pressure cooker, allowing steam to vent harmlessly before it builds up to dangerous levels and explodes.

When applied to anger and relapse, time-out serves a similar function. This coping skill can *temporarily* put distance between you and risk factor(s) threatening to activate the anger–relapse cycle. Once at a safe distance, you can review available options and pick the response choice most likely to prevent relapse and misdirected anger. Since the use of time-out is often associated with acting out behaviors (both in children and adults), by now some of you are thinking, "I'm not explosive, I stuff my anger. This time-out technique will be worthless in my case." That is far from the case. Sometimes subtle expressions of anger (withdrawal, excessive sleep, depression) cause as much or more damage than do more visible forms of anger (yelling, cursing, hitting, throwing, gesturing, and so forth), *especially* when you are at risk for relapse. An example will help illustrate this point.

Think of the plumbing in your house. Most of the pipes are located in the walls, attic, and other hidden areas so they are not visible as we walk through the house. As with thermostats, water pipes sometimes break. These broken pipes can create gushing waterfalls that spew from toilets, sinks, bathtubs, and water mains. This type of leak, although messy, generally gets our immediate attention. Pipes can also break in such a way as to produce slow leaks that may not be noticed for days or weeks. In my current home, we have two bathrooms upstairs. One day I came home from work and found a puddle of water on the kitchen floor below. I looked up at the ceiling and noticed a huge bulge in the sheet rock. When my husband got home he went exploring in the attic and walls of our house. He found considerable damage to the sheet rock and surrounding walls below the broken pipe. The amount of damage indicated this leak was not a new problem, it had just taken awhile before becoming noticeable. In your opinion, which is worse—a slow leak or a major rupture? Both produce damage in varying degrees depending on location and how long they exist before being noticed and repaired. When thinking about time-out, realize that "little or hidden angers" and "tiny cravings" discussed in the previous chapter can create just as much damage as rage and overwhelming craving if ignored.

Still not convinced? Let's look at another example. Think of a tooth with a cavity. Initially, the damage to the tooth is small. If identified and treated early, the tooth suffers little damage. Let's say I am afraid of dentists so put off having it fixed. Six or eight months pass and now I have pain when I chew on the side of my mouth that has the damaged tooth. By the time I go to the dentist most of the tooth is affected. It may require major repairs, a crown, or removal. If I refuse to allow the necessary repairs, my gums or other teeth may be affected. An abscess may develop and as my oral health declines, my general state of health suffers. What started out as a small problem is now jeopardizing my whole body. Ignoring cues that indicate increasing risk for relapse and the misdirection of anger (either inward or outward) lead to a similar outcome. The longer we ignore the obvious, the greater our risk of negative consequences and active relapse.

So how can time-out reduce the risk of relapse and misdirected anger? Before answering this question we must first review the four basic steps of time-out:

1. Decide when you are beginning to get angry.
2. Signal your need to take a time-out.
3. Leave quietly and do something to reduce your anger.
4. Return and discuss the problem with the other person(s) so the conflict can be resolved.

These steps usually work well when your conflict involves a second party with whom you have a stable relationship. You interrupt unproductive conversations by signaling your need to begin a time-out. Next, you take a break, calm down, and think about how to handle the current problem. Finally, you return to jointly resolve the conflict with your partner. What happens when you're dealing with a stranger? What if the other person refuses to cooperate or is drunk or not in their right mind? What if the source of the conflict involves self-directed anger? How can time-out be used to reduce the risk of relapse in high-risk situations? Because the application of time-out in its traditional form is not always possible, the remainder of this chapter will address these very important questions.

How can the time-out technique possibly work with strangers? Well, if you expect to control someone else's behavior it won't! The goal of applying time-out with strangers is to reduce *your* risk of misdirected anger and relapse. Since a stranger might not understand what you are doing if you introduce time-out in its original form, you must creatively apply this technique with the intention of creating opportunities for a successful (or at least a less distressing) outcome. An example might help you better understand this use of time-out.

Say you are at the movie theater waiting to buy your ticket. You have waited patiently in line for 30 minutes. Just as the box office opens, three strangers, who are obviously friends, cut in front of you. Your anger flares but you want to avoid a public scene. Applying the traditional time-out technique is not possible in this setting. Obviously you can't say, "I'm getting angry, I need to take a time-out." They would probably think you were crazy, *plus* you would lose your place in the line if you left to take a time-out. Second, since these people are strangers, you will most likely never see them again, and therefore have no opportunity to return and resolve the conflict. In this type of situation, you must make several decisions about *your own response choices* since the only responses we can control are our own. First, can you remain calm and assertively instruct these individuals to take their proper place in the line? If the answer is no, can you change your thinking so their behavior becomes less personal (i.e., their line cutting was not a personal attack against you. This display of poor manners would have occurred no matter who had been standing there)? Redefining how you view an event reduces the potential for explosive anger or relapse and also for resentment about the event later on (we'll discuss this further in chapter 6). If the answer is no again, what action is necessary to prevent yourself from responding with behavior that creates more problems than it solves (after all, who cares where the blame *really* lies if *you* go to jail for assault or get drunk/high later because you stuffed your feelings and felt victimized)? Time-out in this situation means *actively assuming responsibility for your own behavior regardless of what others say or do*. This is *very* difficult to do so I urge you to weigh the short-lived feeling of self-righteousness against the potentially negative consequences before you decide to respond as you have in the past.

A similar situation arises when conflict involves individuals who are rageful, drunk or high, or not in their right mind. In these instances, applying the traditional time-out technique is a set-up for failure! Individuals who are very angry, high, or not in their right mind are in no position to see logic in anything you say or do. In this case, as in the above situation, the goal is to change your own behavior to avoid feeding into a potentially dangerous situation.

Let's look at another example. I am standing at the bus stop and an obviously drunk individual starts asking me for money and cigarettes. I politely say no and ignore further requests. The individual becomes more insistent, demanding that I give him money and cigarettes, and threatens to "kick my ass" if I don't. Well, if I want to be a tough guy, I can start arguing or simply beat the hell out of him. Unfortunately, I will most likely suffer negative consequences even if technically I am "in the right." A better way to manage this situation, unless the person is physically attacking me, is to remove myself from the setting. This is *not* the same thing as backing down or whimping out! It is simply choosing smart since the other person is in no condition to rationally think about anything.

I know, I know, reading this feels like the sound of nails scratching on a chalkboard! This may be a *very* different approach to how you normally "take care of business," but if your goal is to change *your own behavior* and reduce *your personal risk of relapse*, this is one method for accomplishing this goal. Still, doubtful—well, try it out a few times and see what happens before putting this approach in file 13. Remember what your mother always said about new foods: "Always try it at least once before you say you don't like it."

A third situation requiring modification of the traditional time-out technique involves self-directed anger. How do you tell *yourself* you need to take a time-out because you are disgusted and angry with your own behavior? How do you resolve conflicts with yourself? Do you call forth the old cliché, "me, myself, and I," so there will be more of you to blame? Time-out in this case requires you to interrupt the negative thoughts you use to beat yourself up after making a mistake. It means if you are sitting at home all alone feeling sorry for yourself because your life is such a total waste you pick up the phone and call someone or get busy doing something! The use of a modified version of time-out (taking a break from the thoughts you are experiencing and changing your activity) may keep you from letting this form of "stinking thinking" lead you to relapse or other forms of self-destructive behavior.

Finally, how can time-out reduce the risk of relapse in high-risk settings? Suppose you go to dinner with a group of friends from work. This group includes some people who know you well enough to be aware of your addiction and others who do not. Some of the newer group members order drinks, offering to buy a round for the table. This creates quite a dilemma, especially if your sobriety is new or shaky! Applying a modified version of time-out can buy you the time needed to maintain your sobriety. In this instance, you would simply extend your regrets and leave the setting. After you leave, call someone, such as your sponsor, who can help you process your feelings about this event.

You can approach this problem from several directions. One option would be to come up with a positive way to approach newer group members and alert them of your need to avoid high-risk situations (sitting at a table where alcohol is being consumed by others). This may or may not include asking members to refrain from drinking when you are out with the group. A second option would be to identify other activities the group could participate in that do not include the presence of alcohol (Sunday brunch at a cafeteria that does not serve alcoholic beverages). A third option would be to alert group members that you may have to leave suddenly if you sense your risk of relapse increasing. This way you can still participate on some level but won't startle others if you suddenly disappear. Finally, you might feel angry and resentful but say nothing and just see what happens (certainly not *my* favorite option)! As you can see, there are as many options as you have creative ideas.

I hope by now you are convinced to at least give time-out a try. A good way to start is to apply the traditional time-out technique to situations involving family and friends. Teach them the steps in this process and explain why you are using it (in case you don't know, the answer is to improve the way you and those you love handle conflict and to reduce your relapse potential). As your skill in using time-out increases, gradually begin applying modified versions. Although practice does not make perfect, it can increase your skill in successfully applying new behaviors. If you use this technique regularly, you will discover that it works more than it fails. Finally, the success rate of time-out is even higher when combined with detouring self-talk, the topic of chapter 6. Since thoughts have a tremendous impact on feelings and behavior, learning to redirect negative thinking, within the context of time-out, is an important cornerstone for recovery.

6

Mind Games

When I wake up, my mind automatically begins to think about the upcoming day. A typical conversation with myself runs like this: "I hope Vincent is in a good mood and cooperates when I get him ready for daycare. Oh! I better put something out for dinner. I hope the freeways are running smooth. I wonder how many new patients were admitted last night. I sure hope the weather stays pretty so I can walk after work."

This private conversation is referred to as "self-talk." It is the back-and-forth chatter we have with ourselves as we go through each day. Self-talk is how our minds make sense of the things we call daily life. Self-talk is so common that we rarely pay it any mind on a conscious level. On the surface, self-talk seems pretty harmless. After all, thinking about our daily life helps us organize and move through it with less stress—*right*?

Well now, that all depends! It depends on whether the self-talk has a positive or negative focus. The chatter I presented above is pretty neutral and doesn't affect my mood too much one way or the other. Let's look at these statements with a positive and then a negative twist to see what happens.

Positive self-talk: "I bet Vincent will be in a great mood today, he's such a good little boy. Oh! I'll make tacos for dinner. Its quick and easy and everybody *loves* tacos! I hope the freeways are clear today. If not, maybe I'll get a chance to listen to my new CD. I hope the new admissions are interesting, I wonder how many there were. I hope the weather is pretty so I can walk after work. If not I can always go to the mall and window shop while I walk."

Negative self-talk: "I can't believe I had another baby! Why did I put myself in such a bind. Life would be so much easier without children! How come I always have to cook dinner? I wish I could come home just once and have somebody cook for me. Oh God! It's Monday! I bet the freeways will be jammed with maniacs today. I bet all the new admissions are bad actors. With my luck today will be a disaster. It'll probably rain like hell today since I want to walk so bad. I sure don't want to walk in the mall, it's so crowded!"

Can you believe all that stuff?! A self-talk conversation of 5 or 10 minutes can produce lots of material. Look closely at the positive and negative self-talk examples above. How I choose to organize my thinking *greatly* influences my physical reactions, emotional state, and behavior. Positive self-talk reduces stress, improves my mood, and generally leads me to respond to others and my environment in a positive manner. Negative self-talk increases stress level, depresses my mood, and contributes to defensive, guarded behavior.

Since all of us want our lives to be as happy and stress free as possible, why would anyone *consciously* choose to apply negative self-talk? The answer is *they wouldn't*! Remember, self-talk is a process we develop early in life that becomes as natural as breathing. Most of us never stop to question what we are thinking and how it affects us. Negative self-talk generates the same effect on the anger–relapse cycle that kerosene has on a campfire. If you are standing too close, you can get serious burns from the chemical reaction that occurs when the match hits the kerosene. That's why forest rangers always warn people *not* to start fires that way! Negative self-talk seriously increases the potential for misdirected anger and relapse. Let's look at an example to see this process in action.

Max worked hard at the office today. Driving home, he was almost rear-ended on the freeway. As he turns into his driveway, he sees that his daughter's tricycle is thrown carelessly across the driveway. He has to get out and move it before parking the car. When he walks in the door his daughter is crying. His wife tells him there is a bill he needs to review *now* and that the yard needs mowing *before* dinner. The nature of

Max's self-talk will significantly influence the outcome of this truly challenging day.

If Max applies positive self-talk, his internal conversation might go something like this: "Well, my day certainly has been challenging! I guess it can only go up from here. I'll let my wife know I need a few minutes to regroup and then I'll start tackling problems. Life in the fast lane!" The outcome will be *very* different if Max elects to apply negative self-talk: "Who the hell does that _____ think she is demanding that I look at bills and mow the grass after the kind of day I just had! She didn't even make Jane pick up her tricycle she's so irresponsible! My job sucks, my family sucks, and life sucks! I'll have a few drinks so I can cope with all this chaos!"

Remember this self-talk occurs silently inside your head so nobody is the wiser—*until you open your mouth!!* If your self-talk is negative, I *guarantee* you will either withdraw and refuse to talk at all, start screaming and yelling, or resort to substance abuse and blame others for your behavior. This is why it is so important to become familiar with your personalized pattern of self-talk. Once you identify the direction of your self-talk you can develop coping skills to replace negative self-talk with more productive options. When positive self-talk is added to the time-out technique described in chapter five, your risk of relapse and misdirected anger drops dramatically.

Okay, I can hear you now: "Jo, you're *nuts!!* You must live in a dream world. Nobody can really learn to change their thinking like that! You've been watching too many reruns of *Leave It to Beaver*. (This is a *great* example of negative self-talk!). I *never* said it would be easy! Learning to redirect your self-talk is one of the hardest techniques to learn but probably the most important. Yes, it takes a lot of energy to identify and change self-talk, but how much energy do you use trying to *undo* all those hostile responses and episodes of relapse that make you feel about two inches high!?

If you are *really* serious about learning how to manage your anger and avoid relapse, this chapter will give you the *beginning* ingredients to put this process in action. A word of caution before we get started. Remember the road you traveled to create your current pattern of self-talk was a long one. This road is the same distance in the opposite direction! It takes time, commitment, and ongoing effort to alter lifelong patterns of thinking. You will experience successes, but setbacks, especially when you are stressed, tired, or confronted with those surprise events we call "life," also occur. Be aware that setbacks are just the kerosene you need to convince yourself to abandon treatment and blame *me* when things go wrong. "I knew this stuff wouldn't work. That Jo Clancy really *is* nuts!" I invite you to *at least* give it a try! You have nothing to lose and everything to gain. After all, you can *always* go back to negative self-talk if you decide change is more trouble than it's worth.

Self-talk is a difficult concept for people to understand. How do individuals develop a particular style of thinking about life events? How does this internal chatter then influence our daily lives? These questions deserve further examination before techniques designed to redirect self-talk are introduced. One way to explain how self-talk develops is to look at childhood experiences. Each of us receives certain messages in childhood that we "buy into" and continue to replay in adulthood. Rare is the day that any one of us stops to consider whether the messages that shaped and continue to guide the direction of our self-talk are sensible or obsolete! An example might help you better understand this approach.

My grandmother is 90 years old. She has seen many changes during her lifetime: the invention of television, motorized vehicles, airplanes, rocket ships, computers, automatic washers and dryers, and so on. As technology and my grandmother's age advance, she becomes increasing bewildered and set in her ways. My aunt and uncle installed cable television for her birthday one year thinking this would please her. They were disappointed when she said, "I would rather stick with regular television if it's all the same to you." Her childhood belief was to keep life as simple as possible. This "fit" in her youth since she was a busy farm girl with little time for the "frills" in life. Things have changed a great deal since she was a young woman; however, she continues to believe that simple equals better. Although this belief doesn't always fit her current situation (i.e., modern technology could make her life easier and more interesting now her ability to get around is limited), she simply cannot accept the fact that different might be better.

The state of our self-esteem also plays a role in the direction of self-talk. Feeling happy, confident, and loved creates positive self-talk, increasing our sense of self-worth. This positive view of ourselves and the world gives rise to more positive self-talk, reducing our risk of misdirected anger and relapse. On the contrary, feeling sad, confused, frightened, and angry, and not knowing what to do with these feelings, creates negative self-talk, seriously eroding self-esteem. Because low self-esteem is the primary side-effect of negative self-talk, and negative self-talk fuels low self-esteem, this process becomes a primary trigger in the activation of the anger–relapse cycle.

When addiction is involved, self-esteem is further damaged by the presence of shame and the unspoken rules that govern addictive behavior: "Don't talk, don't trust, don't feel." These factors generate sadness, confusion, and anger that in turn activate negative self-talk: "I'm no good; it's too late to change; who would notice anyway; if only. . . ." This can also occur in the opposite direction. Say I experience something positive that most people would find uplifting. If I am an addict or alcoholic, feeling positive creates feelings of guilt, confusion, and anger. These feelings, in turn, give rise to negative self-talk: "I don't deserve this; this is too good to be true; when is the other shoe going to drop." Unless interrupted, the individual will ultimately resort to substance abuse to alleviate guilt and confusion.

Feelings, thoughts, self-esteem, and behavior are all ingredients in our personalized patterns of response. With this in mind, let's move on to the three primary purposes of this chapter: (1) recognizing negative self-talk; (2) identifying the impact it has on self-esteem and recovery; and (3) developing strategies to interrupt this process.

The first step involves identifying faulty beliefs that feed the anger–relapse cycle. Each of you has a set of beliefs that were acquired in childhood. Refer back to worksheet 1 where you identified the patches on your quilt. These patches, based on the spoken and unspoken messages you received from those around you, created beliefs that shaped and continue to influence your worldview. Your worldview gave rise to the triggers that activate physical, emotional, cognitive, and behavioral cues. If the messages were positive, you probably developed a favorable self-image and sense of fair play in dealing with life on life's terms. If, however, these messages were negative, a disapproving self-image and resistance to accepting life on life's terms was the predictable result. Because beliefs based on negative messages damage self-esteem and increase the risk of relapse and misdirected anger, they must be identified and challenged before self-talk can be successfully redirected.

How do you identify whether your beliefs are based on positive or negative messages? Worksheet 1 and your anger journal are a good place to start. These two activities (*provided you completed the worksheet and have been keeping your journal—if not, do it NOW!!*) identify the messages you received during childhood and the triggers and cues they created and continue to fuel. Review your worksheet and journal, paying close attention to the negative messages you identified as stemming from childhood events. Now, carefully examine these messages and see if they "fit" at this point in your life. This is an important process since we rarely challenge fixed beliefs, no matter how senseless, unless someone, like a therapist, invites us to. Examples might include:

> "I've been a loser from the word go, it's too late for me to change."
> "What's the point of changing? I can never please everyone so might as well focus on pleasing myself."
> "Drugs and alcohol are really a form of self-medication. It's the only way I can cope with my feelings."
> "My anger is the only thing that keeps me alive, if I stop being angry, I'll die."
> "Why should I learn to redirect *my* anger, nobody else does!"

Exposing faulty beliefs created by negative childhood messages, and their damaging effect on self-esteem and the recovery process, is critical. Otherwise, existing patterns of feeling, thinking, and behaving will feed the vicious cycle of self-blame, anger, and relapse. An example will illustrate how to begin this process of self-discovery. Although the following story is made up, it could easily represent the life of a real person.

Jane Doe was born the fifth of five children. She was a midlife "surprise" to her parents whose other children were teenagers and young adults. Jane's parents never told her she was unwanted; however, their behavior sent negative messages that had a devastating effect on her self-esteem. Jane's parents rarely held or kissed her. They tended to her basic needs but spent little time talking to or playing with her. By the time Jane was a teenager, she craved affection and often felt lonely and unloved. She became sexually active in a desperate attempt to obtain the love she so frantically needed. She also began using drugs and alcohol to cope with her emotional pain.

When Jane was 30, her best friend threw a party. She was very excited about how much fun this event would be—but never received an invitation. Instead of calling her friend to ask why she had not been included, Jane went on a drug and alcohol binge that nearly resulted in her death. Jane's negative self-talk "my friend doesn't love me; I must be even more worthless than I thought; nobody will ever *really* love me," prevented her from approaching her friend for an explanation, which in this case was that an invitation had been sent but lost in the mail.

Reviewing this event, we learn that the source of Jane's negative self-talk was the unspoken messages she received in childhood. This transfer of unspoken messages (from Jane's parents) into beliefs of the next generation (Jane's unconscious interpretation of these messages), was so subtle, that it occurred without their conscious awareness. Since we rarely challenge our beliefs, or their origin, they continue to influence feelings, thoughts, self-esteem, and behavior creating real-life situations like the make-believe story of Jane Doe. Identifying and reviewing existing beliefs, especially those flowing in a negative direction, is the first step in redirecting negative self-talk messages.

I hope by now you are beginning to understand the importance of identifying and interrupting patterns of negative self-talk. A second, equally challenging task awaits us once we identify these patterns: *We must accept responsibility for personal response choices, regardless of how we feel and think, or what others say and do!* The faulty belief, "When my life does not go as planned, it's not *my* fault I abuse substances and misdirect my anger," must be challenged and replaced with the more constructive belief: "Life may not always turn out as planned; however, I can learn to recognize the feelings and thoughts these situations create and take action to reduce my risk of relapse and misdirected anger." See models 4 and 5 for a visual review of positive and negative self-talk in action.

Do these models look vaguely familiar? Well, they *should*! Refer back to chapter 1 where models of high and low relapse potential were introduced. Look closely and you will discover that self-talk plays a significant role in the anger–relapse cycle. Negative self-talk damages self-esteem creating a sense of powerlessness. This generates episodes of misguided anger and relapse. Positive self-talk increases self-esteem, creating a sense of personal competence that allows you to interrupt this cycle. The ability to redirect self-talk is vital to every technique presented in this book. Until you make a firm commitment to monitor and redirect negative self-talk, efforts to redirect anger and reduce the risk of relapse will not be effective no matter how many times you read this book!

Model 4: Positive Self-Talk and the Road to Recovery

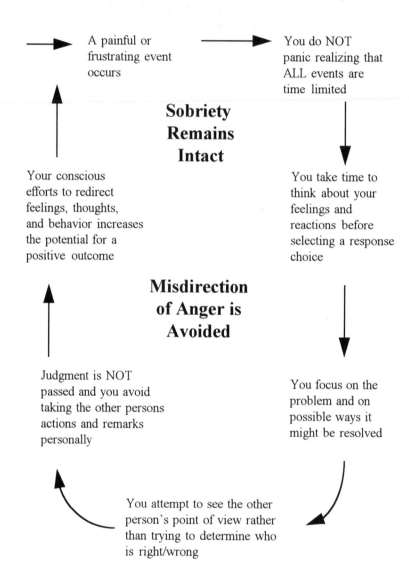

A painful or frustrating event occurs

You do NOT panic realizing that ALL events are time limited

Sobriety Remains Intact

Your conscious efforts to redirect feelings, thoughts, and behavior increases the potential for a positive outcome

You take time to think about your feelings and reactions before selecting a response choice

Misdirection of Anger is Avoided

Judgment is NOT passed and you avoid taking the other persons actions and remarks personally

You focus on the problem and on possible ways it might be resolved

You attempt to see the other person's point of view rather than trying to determine who is right/wrong

Model 5: Negative Self-Talk and the Road to Relapse

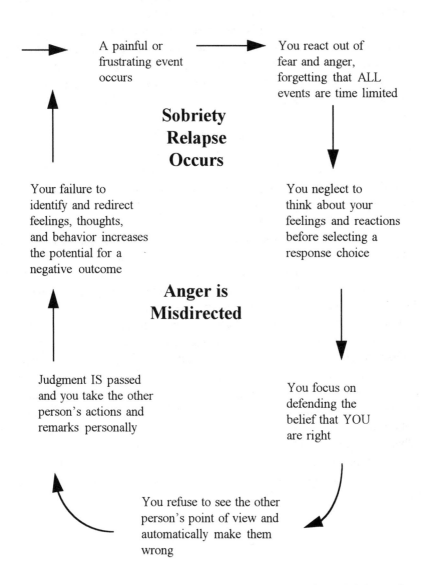

A painful or frustrating event occurs

You react out of fear and anger, forgetting that ALL events are time limited

Sobriety Relapse Occurs

Your failure to identify and redirect feelings, thoughts, and behavior increases the potential for a negative outcome

You neglect to think about your feelings and reactions before selecting a response choice

Anger is Misdirected

Judgment IS passed and you take the other person's actions and remarks personally

You focus on defending the belief that YOU are right

You refuse to see the other person's point of view and automatically make them wrong

A final exercise provides opportunities for you to begin identifying and challenging negative self-talk messages. The exercise itself generates a host of self-talk that will try to talk you out of completing this activity: "This is *so* stupid, does she really think anyone will do this?" "This is so silly, I'm much too busy to sit in front of a mirror making faces at myself!" Resist the urge to avoid this exercise—it just might teach you something about yourself you need to know. Remember, you have nothing to lose and everything to gain—*go for it*! The name of this exercise is the *egg-timer technique*.

The next time you feel angry or upset, take an egg timer and sit in front of a mirror. Make sure the mirror is in a location free from distractions. Set the egg timer for 5 minutes and proceed to tell yourself *out loud* all the negative feelings and thoughts you are experiencing. Pay special attention to your tone of voice, the gestures and facial expressions you use, and what happens to your anger as the exercise progresses. When 5 minutes have passed, reset the timer, and replace your negative feelings and thoughts with positive affirmations. Again, notice your tone of voice, the gestures and facial expressions you use, and what happens to your anger. Pay attention to the negative self-talk that creeps in as you say the affirmations: "This is *really* stupid, I feel like a fool!" "What good will this do in the real world?" "I can't believe I'm actually doing this!"

Negative messages, like the ones identified above, undermine positive feelings and thoughts. This reinforces the belief that you are doomed to experience only heartache and misery for the rest of your life. When you finish the egg-timer technique, write down feelings, thoughts, and impressions that occurred before, during, and after the exercise. Use this technique as often as necessary and review the results on a regular basis. What is the point of all this? First, to increase your awareness of negative self-talk and its effect on your recovery. Second, and of equal importance, to challenge and begin replacing self-defeating messages with more productive alternatives.

7

Which Way Does Your Lava Flow?

In previous chapters we learned that past experiences, triggers, cues, and self-talk play an important role in how we feel, the state of our self-esteem, and how we ultimately choose to behave. We discovered that links exist between childhood events and factors that later become triggers and cues. We also learned that self-talk flows in two directions: positive and negative, creating dramatically different results. Positive self-talk produces assertive responses. That means we take responsibility for identifying and expressing our feelings and needs to others. Negative self-talk, like kerosene on a campfire, encourages stuffing, passive explosions, or aggressive acting out—*all* guaranteed to bring about episodes of misdirected anger and relapse! Learning to recognize your personal patterns of response, and redirect responses that do not serve you well, is the focus of this chapter.

There are four basic styles of response: passive, assertive, passive–explosive, and aggressive. Each individual has a primary pattern of response that influences communication with others. Although fairly stable across time, response styles can shift, temporarily or permanently, depending on where we are, whom we are with, and what is occurring in our lives. The state of our self-esteem, and how past experiences and self-talk messages play themselves out in the here-and-now, also affects response choices. A closer look at the four basic styles of response will help you understand how each is created and maintained across time (see model 6 and table 1). As you read the following material, remember the goal is to identify *your personalized pattern of response choices* by the end of this chapter!

"Still waters run deep" is a good way to describe *passive responses*. On the surface things appear smooth and calm but underneath—look out for rocks and branches! Individuals whose primary style of response is passive, "swallow their feelings" avoiding any direct mention of their discomfort. This creates a sense of confusion for others who "know" *something* is wrong but cannot figure out what. Passive responses place others in the awkward position of trying to "second guess" what you think and feel. They inevitably guess wrong! Resentments arise and become excellent excuses to end relationships, drink and use drugs, or participate in other forms of self-destructive behavior all the while silently blaming others. Since "the problem" is never openly identified there is little hope of a successful outcome. The result: damaged self-esteem (if I was really worth anything they would have known what I wanted/needed), negative feelings, thoughts, behavior, and relapse!

Since passive responses lead to unmet needs, frustration, a sense of helplessness, and isolation from those we need the most, why do people choose to communicate in this manner? The answer: *THEY DON'T—at least not consciously!* Think back to the patches on your quilt. Several types of childhood experiences can create this pattern of response. Individuals with family histories of verbal, emotional, sexual, or physical abuse learned to be quiet and small so the abuse would stop more quickly. Unfortunately, when they reach adulthood these patterns continue, even when no threat of abuse is present. Painful memories of past childhood events, stored in the unconscious mind, continue to activate passive responses.

A second childhood experience that contributes to passive responses is membership in a chemically dependent family. Members of these families quickly learn to stuff feelings and avoid conflict at all cost. This style of communication "teaches" individuals that if feelings remain unspoken family reactions will remain uncomfortable but predictable. This pattern continues until a crisis forces one or more members to break the silence and challenge the existing situation. Without treatment, even

Model 6: The Four Basic Response Styles

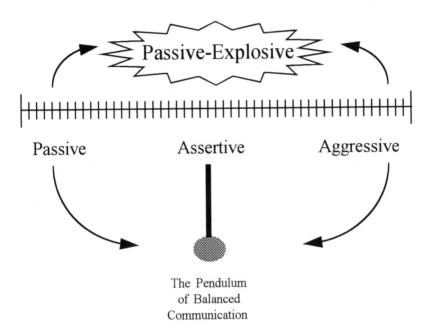

The Pendulum
of Balanced
Communication

those who "escape" their families will create the same pattern of response in other relationships.

Finally, one's culture, and the beliefs and values it promotes, can encourage passive behavior. Certain groups of people have strong cultural values that discourage assertive behavior. There is a certain "pecking order" that places people in fixed positions in social and family relationships. Although this does not create problems in their own cultural group what happens when this person interacts with individuals from other cultural backgrounds? Let's look at an example. When I was a graduate student I had a classmate from Saudi Arabia. She told me that in her country women were commanded to cover their entire body, including their face, when in public. She was also forbidden to drive a car, and had few rights to participate in political activities. She enjoyed the freedom American women have to speak, dress, and behave as they

Table 1
The Four Basic Styles of Response

Passive	Passive–Explosive	Assertive	Aggressive
Swallows feelings and silently seethes inside	Swallows feelings and later becomes explosive during unrelated events	Openly expresses feelings using "I" messages "When you ＿＿ I feel ＿＿ because ＿＿. What I would like in the future is ＿＿"	Explosively expresses feelings by threatening, cursing, gesturing, physical contact
Avoids healthy confrontation at all costs and justifies this behavior by thinking, "If I wait long enough, the other person will surely figure out what they did wrong and correct it"	Avoids healthy confrontation and justifies this avoidance by thinking, "Surely the other person will figure this out. If not, there will be hell to pay later!"	Focuses on personal reactions. Identifies the problem at hand and openly seeks strategies to bring about productive resolution	Confrontation is one-sided and self-destructive. The focus is on proving your point and showing the other person just how wrong they are
Blames others for not figuring out what they feel, want, and need. Uses this as an excuse to drink, use drugs, end relationships	Blames others and harbors resentments that later emerge as "rage attacks" and relapses	Avoids assigning blame to self or others when things go wrong. Attempts to listen to and understand everyone's point of view	Blames others and initiates action to "make the other person pay" for their behavior. This fosters resentments in others and leads to communication breakdowns.
Prevents problem resolution. What is not identified cannot be addressed	Greatly reduces the possibility of problem resolution. Avoidance and explosions are poor motives for cooperation	Increases the potential for problem resolution by creating an atmosphere of mutual trust and respect	Prevents problem resolution and increases conflict and isolation
Damages self-esteem and fosters negative feelings, thoughts, and behaviors	Damages self-esteem and fosters negative feelings, thoughts, and behaviors	Increases self-esteem and fosters positive feelings, thoughts, and behaviors	Damages self-esteem and fosters negative feelings, thoughts, and behavior
High Relapse Potential	*High Relapse Potential*	*Reduced Relapse Potential*	*High Relapse Potential*

Note: Adapted from *Anger and addiction: Breaking the relapse cycle, a teaching guide for professionals*, by J. Clancy, 1996. Madison, CT: Psychosocial Press.

choose and participated in these customs while in America. She was, however, very clear that once she returned home her former pattern of passive behavior would be necessary to achieve family and social acceptance.

This leads us into another important area of discussion: since passive behavior in American culture is generally seen as negative, are there circumstances when it is the *best* pattern of response? The answer is *yes!* Passive behavior is essential when you are dealing with a drunk, high, or extremely rageful person. Yes, you can put on your "tough person routine" but it may get you killed! If someone were holding a gun to my head, I would not become aggressive and demand they put the gun down. Trying to be assertive—"When you put a gun to my head, I feel scared and angry. I feel this way because I think you are going to kill me. What I would like is for you to put the gun down"—would also be a dangerous response. The best option would be to bide my time and see what unfolds. I can always become aggressive later if all else fails.

When visiting places where cultural beliefs are very different from our own, respect for the dignity of others dictates that we follow local rules and behaviors. When I visited Israel last year I experienced several very different cultural norms. First, Israeli women are much more passive than American women. They dress more modestly and do not draw attention to themselves in public, therefore, I followed suit. In contrast, Israel has been in conflict over religious issues for centuries creating an atmosphere of tension. Armed soldiers were on the buses, at checkpoints along the road, in museums, restaurants, and everywhere else I went. Although this appeared very aggressive and hostile by American standards, it was actually an attempt to maintain a passive existence between different cultures all trying to find their place in one society.

Although passive responses can be valuable in certain circumstances, they are poison in personal relationships! Any ongoing relationship, be it with family members, friends, or coworkers, occasionally experiences conflict. This is normal and healthy since we cannot always agree on issues. The best strategy for managing conflict is to assertively state your feelings, allow the other person to express theirs, and work together to resolve the conflict (chapter 8 will provide an in-depth look at this issue). I know, this is hard to believe! You have *always* believed that if you just "shut-up" things will work themselves out. Well, what happens is the opposite. The problem continues to grow and what could have been resolved with relative ease becomes a major obstacle in the relationship. Let's look at an example.

Sue and Bill (not their real names) had been married 25 years. Bill was an alcoholic who refused to stop drinking. In the early years of their marriage, Sue expressed her concern and discomfort with this behavior. Each time Sue tried to tell Bill her feelings, she ran into a wall of resentment. As the years passed, Sue "learned" that it was easier to be quiet about Bill's drinking. She worked hard to create a "normal" life for her family. Her resentment and frustration, however, continued to grow with each passing day. Finally, Sue announced to Bill that she wanted a divorce. Bill was devastated, stating, "I never knew the problem was that serious." He offered to stop drinking and enter treatment, but it was too late. Sue's anger and sense of hopelessness about the marriage made it impossible for this couple to work out their differences. If Sue had taken a more assertive stance (attended Alanon, asked for a temporary separation and attended counseling, stopped covering for Bill each time his drinking interfered with his ability to function), this marriage might have been saved. I know, there are no guarantees, but the fact that Sue "swallowed" her feelings for all those years led to such a buildup of resentment that no amount of professional intervention could save the marriage—it was simply too late.

What happened to Bill and Sue is a good example of how best intentions often produce the opposite result. Sue thought if she was patient that Bill would eventually "come to his senses" and stop drinking. Bill thought that since Sue had stopped complaining, that his drinking was no longer a problem in the relationship. Neither partner was at fault, but the consequences for both were severe. The erosion of trust and love progressed so far that it could not be reversed. Just like a cavity in a tooth, once the decay reaches a certain point, the tooth, and in this case Bill and Sue's marriage, cannot be saved.

Let's look at a second example. Bob (not his real name) was the oldest of three sons. There had always been competition between Bob and his younger brothers and the youngest brother often made comments that Bob found hurtful and offensive. Bob never told his younger brother how these comments affected him, so this behavior continued well into their adulthood. One Sunday, Bob and his brothers were all having dinner with their parents. Bob told the family he was in a recovery program for alcoholics and was pleased to announce he had achieved 6 months of sobriety. True to form, his younger brother made the comment, "Gee, Bob, how long will it last *this time?*" This comment was very painful for Bob, but he ignored it and swallowed his feelings. There was an awkward silence at the table and then someone else moved on to a safer topic. That was the last family dinner Bob ever attended. Twenty years passed and he avoided his family making excuses each time he was invited to dinner. If Bob had stated his feelings early on this conflict might have provided the family with an opportunity to strengthen their relationships instead of resulting in Bob's withdrawal from the family.

Again, as in the marriage of Bill and Sue, neither Bob nor his family members were to blame. Bob lacked the skills to assertively state his feelings, so did the only thing he felt he could—withdraw from further painful comments. His family, bewildered by Bob's withdrawal from all family functions, did not know how to respond. Therefore, they took no action to directly confront the problem. In both examples, the parties involved lacked skills to assertively state their feelings and needs. They were so afraid of being rejected that they created self-fulfilling prophecies.

At the opposite end of the scale are *aggressive responses*. Individuals whose main response style is aggressive become hostile and defensive when attempting to make a point. Afraid of not being taken seriously, they yell, curse, make gestures, and sometimes resort to physical violence. Like peacocks, they spread their feathers and run around trying to look colorful. Unfortunately, they create the image of a porcupine with its quills outspread ready to attack. Their inability to express thoughts and feelings generates resistance in others, reducing the likelihood of successful problem resolution. Resentments and a desire to "get even" are common and often lead to breakdowns in communication, damaged self-esteem, and relapse.

If aggressive responses create such an atmosphere of hostility and resentment, then why would anyone consciously choose this style of response? Just as we discovered with passive responses, they wouldn't! Aggressive responses also stem from childhood experiences that, unless interrupted, influence our interactions with others throughout our lives. Several childhood experiences play a role in this process. Being reared in a home with physical, emotional, verbal, or sexual abuse can create a pattern of aggressive response. When individuals reach the fork in the road between passive or aggressive behavior, they *subconsciously* think about all they have lost through aggressive acts of others. They make a vow to themselves that *nobody* will ever take advantage of them again. Unfortunately, as with passive responses, these patterns are carried into adulthood and applied when there is no need for aggression.

A second childhood experience, resembling that of passive behavior, is being reared in a chemically dependent family. If you are never allowed to openly express feelings and needs in your family you find other outlets for anger and frustration. Again, this process is unconscious and individuals are rarely aware of the reason for their aggressive responses. One goal of therapy involves helping aggressive individuals look beneath their mask of anger to identify what they are truly feeling. They generally discover poor self-esteem, a fear of rejection or abuse, and confusion regarding how to more productively let others know how they think and feel.

Finally, an individual's cultural background, and the beliefs and values it promotes, play a role in the development of aggressive responses. Some cultures are much more aggressive than others out of necessity. When I traveled to Egypt, I visited the city of Cairo which has 15 million inhabitants. Since poverty is widespread in Egypt, and resources scarce, aggressive responses may mean the difference in keeping food on the table. My husband and I went to the Cairo Bazaar and I was astounded by the aggressive behavior of store clerks. They touched, gestured, pleaded, and generally harassed everyone who passed by their shops. I attempted to say no politely, and then became very assertive, stating, "I am not interested, please go away!" This response created the opposite response—the clerk chased me down the street and demanded I sample his wares. I was forced to become verbally aggressive, cursing and gesturing, before he finally gave up and retreated. Although this behavior was uncomfortable for me, it is typical in Egypt and the clerk was not even offended. The message here is that we must view an individual's responses in context. This means we need to carefully look around us so we can determine if aggressive behavior is "normal" or "abnormal" based on the person's cultural background and setting. At the Cairo Bazaar, aggressive responses were *essential* to self-preservation since many clerks are competing for the tourist dollars. In this setting, passive or assertive responses might lead to starvation.

Although aggressive responses are *generally* viewed negatively in American culture, are there circumstances when this style of response is the preferred choice? Again, as with passive behavior, there are exceptions to every rule. If you are a soldier in combat, failure to become aggressive will result in the deaths of yourself and others. If you are attacked aggressive behavior may be your only hope for survival. Finally, as I learned in Egypt, when you interact with certain cultural groups, aggressive responses are not only necessary but expected.

As demonstrated above, there are justifiable reasons to resort to aggression. In personal relationships, however, this response style can only result in negative consequences. When we try to control others, the predictable outcome is hostility and resistance. Think about *your own reaction* when someone demands that you say or do a certain thing. The typical response is to do just the opposite! Let's look at an example.

Sam and Mary (not their real names) have been married 15 years. They have a long-standing pattern of verbally abusing each other. Sam often threatens to choke Mary unless she shuts up, which leads Mary to become even more verbally abusive. One day the couple had a fight about an upcoming family event and the verbal abuse became particularly vicious. Sam told Mary that she had 10 seconds to shut up or he would choke her until she had no choice but to shut up. She responded by taunting Sam and daring him to choke her "if you are man enough." Sam, lacking the skills to apply time-out, did indeed choke Mary until she almost passed out. This event scared them so badly they sought counseling.

This is a good example of communication gone haywire. Neither partner was wrong, they simply lacked the skills to defuse their pattern of aggressive responses. In therapy they learned to apply time-out and positive self-talk to avoid "feeding into" each other's hostile comments. Both partners were assisted in identifying what they truly wanted to express to each other, and were taught to use assertive responses to express feelings and thoughts more productively. They learned to identify their buildup process and apply their new skills before it increased to a point of verbal abuse or physical violence.

Passive–explosive responses are a third style of response choices. This style of communication is a combination of passive and aggressive responses. Individuals with this style of response swallow their feelings. They irrationally believe that if they wait long enough, the other person will figure out what they have "done wrong" or "overlooked" and correct it. The flaw in this line of thinking is that others have little chance of identifying, much less modifying, their own behavior when they don't even know what the problem is! This approach is similar to having a thought and asking someone else to "guess" what you are thinking. Unless a crystal ball is close by they will certainly guess wrong! The frustration level of passive exploders continues to increase across time. Eventually, they reach a breaking point and explode with verbal, emotional, or physical attacks on the "target" of their frustration. These rage attacks are usually triggered by some small event that is not even related to the source of their original anger. This dramatic behavior leaves the other party feeling confused and uncertain how to respond. The unfortunate result is a breakdown in communication, damaged self-esteem, and a high risk of relapse.

Again, childhood experiences lead to the development of this response style. Passive exploders are often victims of mixed messages. They hear one thing and experience another so never know quite how to respond. If they are quiet others tease and torment them for being weak. If they become aggressive, they are punished. This confusion generates unconscious efforts to create a response style that others can understand and appreciate. Unfortunately, passive exploders have no models for assertive behavior and tend to overshoot their mark. When they try to state feelings openly, they often leave out important information or come on too strong. This leads to passive–explosive reactions ("I knew I should have just kept my mouth shut. Now it's gone so far that the only way I can get my point across is to be aggressive!").

Are there ever times when passive–explosive behavior is the response pattern of choice? The answer is *yes*! If an individual is at risk for rape, they might first assume an assertive stance (make eye contact, verbally acknowledge the person, run . . .). If cornered, especially if more than one attacker is present, they might assume a passive stance to reduce the risk of serious injury or death. While in a passive mode, the individual would continue to scan the environment for opportunities to escape and might become explosive if an opportunity to escape without great risk of harm were to occur. Another example is a wild animal attack. Think of being in the woods enjoying a walk and suddenly coming upon a mother bear and her cubs. You were out for a pleasure walk so have no weapons with which to defend yourself. The most appropriate response is to drop to your knees and curl up in a face-down position. Once the bear leaves the setting you spring into action and flee to the nearest safe setting to wait until help arrives.

The earlier examples confirm that there are always exceptions where passive, aggressive, and passive–explosive responses are the desired choice. However, in *ongoing personal relationships* passive–explosive responses are guaranteed to create confusion, conflict, and isolation. If relationship partners withdraw and later become explosive about unrelated issues it hardly forms the basis for trusting, intimate interactions. Avoidance and explosions are poor motives for cooperation and mutual respect! So why do people choose this style of response? They don't! It is an unconscious process, created by past experiences and fed with negative feelings, thoughts, behavior, and low self-esteem. The goal of therapy is to help passive exploders identify factors that created and continue this destructive pattern of response. Once awareness is achieved, *conscious choices* can be made to modify self-defeating feelings, thoughts, and behavior. An example will help illustrate this process.

Jane (not her real name) is a single mother with three teenage sons. She has worked hard to help them become independent by teaching them to wash, cook, shop, and clean. Her pet peeve is coming home at the end of the day needing to do her laundry and finding a load of wet clothes in the washer. This is a frequent occurrence since Jane has never told her sons how much this behavior troubles her. One day Jane had a terrible day at work. She'd slept poorly the night before, and her boss placed additional demands on her already overloaded schedule. On the way home she had a flat tire which further contributed to her bad mood. When she arrived home, her sons, on spring vacation, were watching television. As usual, one son's laundry was in the washer interfering with her own washing schedule. Jane had finally had enough! She silently took the clothes out of the washer and placed the sopping wet mess on her son's bed. She did not mention her anger and resigned herself to cooking the family meal. During dinner, Jane's sons asked if they could go to the mall after they finished eating. Jane became enraged, yelling, "You guys are all a bunch of lazy jerks! I work all day, come home and cook dinner, and run around like a chicken with my head cut off, and all you can do is watch television and ask to go to the mall. I wish I had never had children!" All three sons were upset and confused by Jane's behavior. The son whose clothes were in the washer had not yet been upstairs so had no idea this assault stemmed from his failure to finish his laundry before Jane arrived home.

This is a good example of how a small issue can become a major stumbling block in ongoing relationships. Neither Jane nor her sons were "wrong." Teenagers often get caught up in activities and forget to finish laundry and other tasks. Jane, feeling guilty about being a single parent, is reluctant to set too many boundaries lest her sons choose to go live with their father. The use of an assertive statement, "Hey guys, when you leave laundry in the machine I get frustrated because you are home all day and I only have a little time in the evenings to do my laundry. I would really appreciate it if you would please have your washing completed when I get home," would have prevented this massive explosion and saved Jane a lot of silent suffering. It would have also prevented the chaos her outburst created which left her sons feeling confused and angry and Jane feeling inadequate and guilty.

If passive, aggressive, and passive–explosive patterns of response damage ongoing personal relationships, what, then, is the answer? *Assertive responses* are an another option once we learn how to activate them! Assertive responses allow us to openly express feelings and needs *as they arise* instead of waiting for others to magically read our minds. Individuals who practice assertive responses focus on their personal reactions and monitor self-talk messages to identify what they are really feeling. Energy is channeled into identifying and resolving the problem *not* on assigning blame to themselves or others when something goes wrong. Assertive responses allow us to state ideas and opinions and encourage others to do the same. The goal is to work cooperatively so that each person involved in the conflict feels they have been understood and respected. Assertive responses foster mutual respect, increasing the potential for successful problem resolution. They also build self-esteem and promote positive feelings, thoughts, and behavior—the building blocks of recovery.

Well, if assertive responses are so great, why don't people use them more often? Again, refer back to the patches on your quilt. How many of you come from families that said, "Okay kids, let's sit down and practice applying assertive responses." Very few families, if any, formally teach assertive behavior to their children. Assertive responses are an *acquired skill*. We must take active steps to redirect responses assertively. This is a long and difficult process; however, it takes much less energy than repairing all the relationships damaged with passive, aggressive, and passive–explosive responses!

Turn to model 6 which displays the four basic patterns of response. Remember situations do exist that require passive, aggressive, and passive–explosive responses. The goal is to make assertive responses your primary response style in ongoing relationships to encourage intimacy, trust, and mutual respect. Much like the pendulum of a clock, your response choices achieve balance by swinging back to an assertive position. This is vital to the maintenance of sobriety and positive self-esteem.

So, how do you acquire skills necessary to become assertive responders? It involves accepting responsibility for identifying your feelings and needs to others, even when you think they should already know. I am a Master's level therapist married to another Master's level therapist. Do you think we can always identify what the other feels or needs? Of course we can't! *The only way you can guarantee that others know what you are thinking and feeling IS TO TELL THEM!* This raises the question, "Jo, we know assertive responses are the best way to open up the lines of communication, but how do we do it?" The most effective way is to focus on what you feel and need rather than on what the other person has done or not done. The basic steps in this process are:

1. Identify the *specific behavior* that creates your reaction.
2. Clearly state *how you feel* about the other person's behavior.
3. Define *the reason* this behavior disturbs you.
4. *Identify what you would like to have happen* in the future when this issue arises.

Example: When you _____, I feel _____ because _____. What I would like to see happening instead is _____.

I know, I know, you don't believe me! You may have tried this technique in the past and gotten little or no result. Remember, any time you attempt new behaviors there will be starts and stops in the process. You will be shaky at first and others will "test" your sincerity to see what you are really up to. The key is to *consistently* apply "I" messages knowing that people will act out more in the beginning in an attempt to get you to go back to being how you were before. This is normal! Think of how scary it is for you to apply this technique. It is equally scary for your family members, friends, and coworkers to see you doing it. Assertive responses will not always get you what you want but I promise they will create more positive results than negative ones. Although this technique works best in ongoing relationships, when dealing with strangers, the very least that will happen is you will avoid feeding into passive, aggressive, and passive–explosive patterns of response—no matter what the other person does!

The following example clearly demonstrates the importance of assertive behavior. Last year I traveled to Western Australia. Much of this trip was in the outback which contains vast areas of desert and scrub brush. Since fire is always an extreme hazard, the Australian government sets up "controlled burns" to reduce the risk of grass fires. These interventions are designed to burn off scrub brush and block the path of wildfires should one arise. Although controlled burns create damage, their careful placement greatly reduces the damage caused by wildfires.

The application of assertive responses in ongoing relationships produces similar results. Consciously choosing to identify and discuss feelings and needs creates opportunities to redirect conflict before it becomes unpredictable. "I" messages and positive self-talk, like controlled burns in Australia, initially appear harmful since honest communication increases tension by bringing unresolved conflicts into view. Although uncomfortable, it is essential for conflict resolution. In order to resolve problems, we must identify them so involved parties understand the source of irritation. This careful expression of feelings and needs becomes a pathway for mutual respect, cooperation, and trust. Each time assertive responses are applied, your risk of returning to former patterns of passive, passive–explosive, or aggressive behavior decreases. This in turn strengthens relationships and reduces the potential for relapse. Several examples of assertive responses were identified in the stories involving Bob and his brother's hurtful comments, the failure of Bill and Sue's marriage, Sam and Mary's use of assertive skills to productively redirect their responses, and ideas for Jane to more clearly identify what she expected from her sons. Let's look at one final example to firmly set this process in your mind.

In 1992 my husband and I had a baby born 13 weeks early. He spent 4 months in the hospital before coming home. This event completely changed our lives. Our new son required a great deal of care to address his special needs. I was attempting to work, care for my fragile infant, run a house, and have some quality time with my husband and two older sons. As time passed, I felt increasingly overwhelmed and confused. Determined to practice what I teach, I applied assertive responses with good results.

First, I approached my husband stating, "I'm feeling overwhelmed by everything going on in our lives. What I would like is some extra help around the house." He was very supportive and quickly jumped in to take up the slack. Next, I approached my two older sons, then 14 and 16. I said, "When the baby was born, it created a lot of extra stress for all of us. I am feeling very overwhelmed because I just can't get everything done. What I would like is for you guys to take over doing your own laundry and cleaning your rooms and bathroom." They too were fair-minded and pitched in to help.

This assertive style of response created a feeling of team cooperation. It was not "my problem," it was a "family problem." Had I assumed a passive stance, I would have burned out. An aggressive response would have generated hostility and resistance. Finally, a passive–explosive response would have greatly reduced the potential for achieving my desired result (more help in getting things done) because I would not have asked until so overwhelmed I was yelling. Although assertive responses do not guarantee you will *always* get your way, they sure increase the odds of getting at least part of what you want!

The final goal of this chapter is to provide a "hands on" opportunity for you to practice identifying the various patterns of response. Worksheet 3 provides a number of real life situations for you to practice with. Choose what you think is the *best* response for each situation then turn to the answer key to see how you did. Remember, the more you practice, the better you will get at redirecting your responses assertively.

ANGER AND RELAPSE

WORKSHEET 3

PRACTICING RESPONSE STYLES

Read each of the following situations carefully and select the response style you think is being represented. Compare your answers with the answer key once you complete the exercise. (Don't cheat and look first! Remember, the only way you can learn to identify response styles is to practice, practice, practice!)

1. *Mismatched shoes:* Jane bought a pair of shoes at the mall today. When she arrived home, she discovered that the shoes were mismatched (one a size 7 and the other a size 8). Jane returned to the mall and approached the sales clerk stating, "When I arrived home, I discovered my shoes are mismatched. I would really appreciate an exchange and here's my receipt."

Is this style of response:

A. Passive   B. Passive–Explosive
C. Assertive   D. Aggressive

2. *Where's my cheese?* Jill went to the grocery store and purchased a large order of groceries. While putting her groceries away, she discovered her brick of cheddar cheese was missing. She checked the receipt and had indeed been charged for the cheese. Jill was angry but decided not to make a big deal of the missing cheese. She vowed to watch her checker and bagger more closely next time and if they made the same mistake twice, look out!

Is this style of response:

A. Passive   B. Passive–Explosive
C. Assertive   D. Aggressive

3. *The line starts where?* John was at the auto parts store waiting his turn to check out. The line was long and he had been waiting about twenty minutes. It was almost his turn, when suddenly, a younger man cut in front of him. John was angry but chose not to say anything about this incident. He had been in a good mood when he arrived at the store but left feeling angry and abused.

Is this response style:

    A. Passive   B. Passive—Explosive
    C. Assertive   D. Aggressive

4. *Item without a price:* Joe was in the express lane at the supermarket after a long day at work. His order was being processed when the clerk asked, "Do you know how much this package of noodles costs?" Joe did not, so the yellow assistance light was activated for a price check. The woman in line behind Joe began to make negative comments about people getting in the express line without first checking their items for prices. Joe apologized for the inconvenience, but the lady persisted. Finally, Joe could stand no more, grabbed the lady by the arm, and threw her out of the store cursing obscenities behind her.

This style of response is:

    A. Passive   B. Passive—Explosive
    C. Assertive   D. Aggressive

5. *Turn signals, please!* Jennifer was on the freeway during rush hour attempting to arrive in time for a very important meeting. She was in the far left lane when an accident occurred ahead of her which locked up traffic for miles. She put on her turn signal but nobody would let her over. Jennifer began cursing and making obscene gestures at the other drivers. When the freeway cleared, she was so upset she decided to skip work and have a few drinks instead. After all, she deserved a break after all that—right!?

Worksheet 3 (continued)

This style of response is:

A. Passive   B. Passive–Explosive
C. Assertive   D. Aggressive

6. *What happened to my sweater?* Kathy borrowed her sister's sweater without asking and accidentally tore a small hole in it. She was so afraid her sister would be angry that she hid the sweater and denied any knowledge of its whereabouts. As the days went by, Kathy felt more and more guilty about what she had done. She was still too afraid to tell her sister what had happened, but developed a terrible stomach ache that prevented her from attending a major school dance.

This style of response is:

A. Passive   B. Passive–Explosive
C. Assertive   D. Aggressive

7. *The tank is empty:* Randy's wife had a terrible habit of driving the car until it had less than an eighth of a tank of gas. To make matters worse, she did not tell him when the car needed gas, so he was frequently scrambling at the last minute to get gas and avoid being late to work. He never said anything to his wife, but became increasingly angry each time this happened. Finally, his wife approached him one night and asked for a larger grocery allowance. Randy exploded stating, "What the hell is wrong with you! Money is tight enough already. I bet you have enough and misspend it!"

This style of response is:

A. Passive   B. Passive–Explosive
C. Assertive   D. Aggressive

8. *The case of the mildewed towels:* Rick was notorious for using towels and cramming them in his closet. His girl friend would find them days later, sour and mildewed. She attempted to discuss this issue with him in passing and met with the excuse, "Gee, honey, I just get busy and forget." As time passed and the problem continued, Rick's girl friend decided this issue needed resolution before it led to conflicts in the relationship. One night at dinner she said, "Rick, when you leave wet towels in the closet I get really frustrated because they sour and mildew and it makes it very hard for me to get them clean. I would really appreciate it if you would leave your towel on the bathroom floor where I can see it, or put it in the washer so I'll know when it needs to be washed. Rick indicated he was not aware that it had created such an issue, and agreed to at least leave the towel on the bathroom floor.

This style of response is:

A. Passive
C. Assertive

B. Passive–Explosive
D. Aggressive

9. *Muddy shoes, again!?* Ron was the one family member who seemed concerned about the state of the kitchen floor. His wife and children carelessly tracked in mud without even appearing to notice. He made comments about "dirty floors" but never directly stated what he wanted other family members to do about this problem. One day, Ron had just waxed the floors and his "troops" came in tracking mud and leaves. He held his temper but vowed to get even. Later that night Ron went to each family member's closet and took all their shoes. He put them in a bag in the attic and waited until someone discovered their missing shoes. His wife was the first one to notice her shoes were gone, and when she asked what had happened, Ron replied, "I'm sick and tired of all this mess so I took all the shoes. Until the family agrees to take off their shoes at the door, I will continue to take shoes and hide them. You have only two chances, then the shoes go in the garbage—see how you like those apples!"

Worksheet 3 (continued)

This style of response is:

A. Passive   B. Passive–Explosive
C. Assertive   D. Aggressive

10. *Is bedtime really eight o'clock?* Jim and Nancy have a 3-year-old daughter who is determined to set her own bedtime. Nancy has begged, bartered, pleaded, bribed, and threatened, all to no avail. Jim decided to take a different approach. He sat down with his daughter and said, "Kimmy, when you won't go to bed it makes me very sad because you need your sleep to grow big and strong. I want you to go to bed at eight o'clock so you can get plenty of rest, so here's what we'll do. At 7:30 we'll pick up all your toys and get a drink. Then we'll go upstairs and brush your teeth and turn down your bed. Then we'll read a special story together. Just before bedtime we'll rock in the rocking chair as a way to say goodnight." At first Kimmy cried and did not want to go along with this plan. Jim was firm and consistent in keeping to this plan and after several weeks Kimmy looked forward to her bedtime routine.

This style of response is:

A. Passive   B. Passive–Explosive
C. Assertive   D. Aggressive

WORKSHEET 3

ANSWER KEY

1. The correct answer is "C," assertive. Jane was polite and open about the mistake and her need to exchange the shoes. She did not assign blame to herself or the clerk for the error, and resolved the problem as quickly and hassle free as possible.

2. The correct answer is "B," passive—explosive. Jill "stuffed" her feelings but felt angry and taken advantage of. You can bet if the same mistake happens twice, she'll become openly hostile and demanding. A more appropriate way to resolve this problem would be to contact the store by phone and ask to speak to the manager. Jill could then explain the problem to the manager and ask how soon she must return in order for her lost cheese to be replaced. She can also watch the processing of her order more closely next time since human errors do occur.

3. The correct answer is "A," passive. John stood in line for a long time and then allowed the younger gentleman to cut in line without expressing his feelings about this behavior. The other man could have failed to notice John, could have been in a hurry, or could have just been a rude person. An assertive response would have been to say, "Excuse me sir, you must not have noticed me standing here. The end of the line is behind that gentleman over there." If the other person continued to be rude, you must then make a choice about whether this incident merits further action. If you feel it does, enlist the aid of the store clerk or manager to remove yourself from the middle. If after all this action, the younger man remains in front of you, use positive self-talk to redirect your anger. Realize this person has poor manners and most likely has a great deal of trouble in relationships. This incident is not about you personally, it is a reflection of his poor communication skills. In the larger scheme of things, this incident is not worth getting upset about.

Worksheet 3 (continued)

4. The correct answer is "D," aggressive. Joe's behavior was clearly aggressive because he became verbally abusive and touched the other individual. Again, an assertive response might have been to say, "I'm sorry for the inconvenience, but these things happen. I'll be more careful about checking for prices next time." If the woman's abusive behavior continued, Joe could attempt to ignore it. If his own anger continued to escalate, he could have simply left the store without his items. Yes, this is inconvenient, but less inconvenient than going to jail for assault (which is what happened to Joe). Remember, the goal is *not* to change other people's behavior, although this sometimes occurs when we alter our own behavior. The goal is to maintain control of your own responses *no matter what the other person does!*

5. The correct answer is "D," aggressive. Jennifer was clearly aggressive when she began cursing and gesturing at other drivers. She allowed this experience to ruin her whole day and blamed others so she would have an excuse to skip work and have a few drinks. An assertive communication would have gone like this: "I'm feeling very frustrated by all this traffic, but if I'm late, everybody else probably will be too. I might as well put on that new tape I bought and enjoy a little down time. There's no sense getting upset since I can't change the situation anyway." This use of positive self-talk would have allowed Jennifer to defuse her anger and take a more realistic look at her dilemma. It was not life-threatening, and her overreaction only made things worse.

6. The correct answer is "A," passive. Kathy simply pretended the event did not happen. She developed physical symptoms from her guilt that interfered with a major activity. An assertive response would have gone like this: "Hey sis; you'll probably be mad at me but I borrowed your sweater and accidentally tore a hole in it. I know I was wrong to borrow it without asking, and plan to replace it or repair it for you depending on what you prefer. I learned my lesson and will ask next time." Although Kathy's sister will be justifiably angry, her anger will defuse more quickly since her sister is being honest, offering an apology, and offering to repair or replace the sweater. This simple act of honestly admitting a mistake could actually increase positive feelings between these sisters.

7. The correct answer is "B," passive–explosive. Randy has been angry for days and when he finally explodes, it is over a totally unrelated issue. His wife is left feeling defensive and confused since she cannot make a connection between her request for more grocery money and Randy's explosive reaction. A more assertive way for Randy to address the issue of the empty gas tank would be to say, "Honey, when you leave the gas tank of the car on empty and don't tell me, I get really frustrated because by the time I discover I need gas I have to scramble and it starts my day off on the wrong foot. I would really appreciate it if you would either fill up the tank or let me know I need gas so I can leave a little early." This simple response would resolve the problem and there would have been no need to explode about the request for additional grocery money (which was not even the real issue).

8. The answer is "C," assertive. Rick's girl friend indicated her displeasure at finding sour, mildewed towels in the closet. She did not accuse or blame Rick, she simply requested cooperation in resolving this issue. She also gave Rick two choices of where the towel could be left (the bathroom floor or washer) so he had a part in resolving the problem. This nondefensive approach led to positive results that both partners could live with.

9. The correct answer is "B," passive–explosive. Ron's avoidance of directly confronting family members with his displeasure led to drastic measures; holding their shoes hostage with threats to throw them away. This would only increase the potential for family conflict and places Ron at risk of "them" against "me." An assertive way to manage this problem would be to approach the family, say at mealtime when they are all together, and say, "Hey guys, when you track mud and leaves onto my clean floors I get very frustrated and angry. I know its not a big deal to any of the rest of you, but it really bugs me because I put a lot of energy into cleaning the floors. I would really appreciate it if you would leave your shoes in the mud room so the rest of the house will stay clean." This approach requires Ron to "own" his feelings about the muddy floors and identifies it as an issue that he needs "family cooperation" to solve. His chances of getting cooperation, at least most of the time, are high if he uses an assertive response to identify his feelings and needs.

Worksheet 3 (continued)

10. The correct answer is "C," assertive. Jim enlists his daughter's cooperation by making her part of the plan, by having preparation for bedtime become a "family" activity, and by setting consistent and firm limits so she will know he is *really* serious about an eight o'clock bedtime. Clearly stating your feelings and needs, consistently enforcing limits, and asking others for input in the decision-making process always increases the potential for a positive outcome regardless of whether the other person is 3 or 93.

8

Generating Options

Most of us would like to live in a perfect world where life is "hassle free." In this world the house would always be clean, children would always be polite and cooperative, we would all have wonderful jobs, and all of our worries would magically resolve themselves. All of our wants and needs would be met immediately and we would always be on good terms with ourselves and others. Unfortunately, I have yet to discover this stress-free paradise. If you, by chance, stumble across it let me know so I can pack my bags and catch the next plane!

We all know "real life" is far from hassle free. Situations arise every day that challenge us to feel, think, and respond. The choices we make are greatly affected by past experiences (the patches on our quilt) and self-talk messages we create to make sense of life events. These messages shape our beliefs about the world, laying a foundation for what we will later identify as critical wants and needs. When what *is* and what we think *should be* do not agree it creates conflict. This conflict stems from the belief that terrible things will happen if our wants and needs remain unmet. Therefore, getting what we believe is necessary for our well-being is how we attempt to resolve conflict.

There are several flaws in this method of conflict resolution. First, most of us *unconsciously* buy into the belief that *we should always get what we want and need.* If we looked closer at this belief we would realize how unrealistic it is since *nobody always* gets everything they want or need. Since we rarely question our beliefs, the thought "I *deserve* to have all my wants and needs met" increases our desire to get immediate results. It also encourages us to go after what we *imagine* we need without thinking about what long-term consequences our actions might create. The belief that "my needs must be met or life as we know it will cease to exist" creates such dread that we cannot even consider other ways to satisfy our needs. As this process continues, response choices (passive, passive–explosive, or aggressive behavior) are activated and fueled with negative self-talk, further reducing the potential for a successful outcome. An example will help illustrate the consequences of this approach.

Jane (not her real name) came into therapy demanding that the therapist "fix my problems and stop my emotional pain *now!*" Jane felt she had been taken advantage of all her life and was long overdo for her "fair share" of good times. Unfortunately, the patches on Jane's quilt included a square that taught her, "Do unto others before they do unto you, and don't trust anyone because people only help you so they can win your trust and take advantage of you." Jane was unaware of this belief and used verbally aggressive statements to keep others from getting too close. The side effect was that she had few friends, was separated from her family, and felt there was no hope her needs would ever be met. After a number of sessions she was able to identify her primary need "to like myself and feel like my life matters." Jane often blamed others for her failure to feel good about herself and used alcohol to "relieve emotional pain." This created conflict within herself and also with those she most wanted to be close to. Later in this chapter we will apply a problem-solving model to help Jane productively pursue need fulfillment. I think you will be surprised at the outcome!

A second flaw in the quest for need fulfillment is that we forget to consider, "*Why* do I want or need _____ and *why* do I want or need it *now?*" Turn back to worksheet 1 where you identified the patches on your quilt. Review your answers and then write down the self-talk messages that developed as you added patches to your quilt. Think about how these messages shape what you consider to be critical wants and needs. After you complete this process, ask yourself, "Why this, why now?" Your answer will provide a more realistic outlook of your wants and needs and how best to approach and resolve sources of conflict arising from unmet needs. Let's look at another example.

I am rapidly approaching the "big 40" and it has given rise to some interesting thoughts and feelings. When I began writing books 3 years ago I never understood why—now I do! As I reviewed the patches on my quilt, I identified a number of losses involving people I loved who died very young: my father died at 44, my stepfather at 55, my sister at 38, my brother-in-law at 41, my best friend at 27, and my cousin at 32. After reviewing these events, I wrote down my thoughts: "Gee, you'd better get with it—you might not have too much time left!" "It's always better to work ahead—just in case." "There are no guarantees so if you want to make sure you accomplish something, you'd better do it now!"

These self-talk messages created a sense of urgency to hurry up and do it now. I remember at 15 thinking I would live forever; at 25 I could die but probably never would; at 35 my awareness that time really is limited was the fuel I needed to start writing! Knowing this is important because it allows me to keep my perspective, to carefully choose which paths I walk since I can never walk them all in one lifetime. At this point, I decided to write *this* book (I have four others in mind) and enjoy my husband and children. I don't know what my wants and needs will be at 50, but you can bet I will continue to review the patches on my quilt and my self-talk messages to increase the odds of meeting whatever needs I identify!

Finally, when we think about the conflict that arises from unmet wants and needs, our tendency is to blame others. This means that whenever our lives feel out of control, or we don't want to take responsibility for "making things happen or not happen," we find a handy target to get ourselves off the hot seat! This process, like the belief that we should always get what we want or need, is *unconscious*. Until someone teaches us to examine our thoughts and motives for choosing certain responses, we don't even know that choices exist!

The goal of this chapter is to teach you how to recognize and activate options. I know, your self-talk is saying, "Does she really believe this stuff will work? How can I change things since I'm not in control of what others do? That's like asking someone in the back seat to take over while you're going 70 miles an hour on the freeway!" Keep an open mind as you read the following material. You can read it, apply and modify it, and generate some powerful changes in your life. You can also read it and let destructive self-talk messages supply excuses for why it won't work in *your life*! If you choose the second option, I respect your decision, but invite you to explore *why* your current need involves maintaining a course of self-destruction.

Many of you received unspoken messages in childhood instructing you not to share feelings and needs with others. These messages exist in families with substance abuse issues, families lacking effective communication skills, families with a history of verbal, sexual, or physical abuse, and families in which members are divided by death, divorce, or other factors. It is important to remember that individuals in these families care a great deal for each other but lack the ability to show their feelings. This creates the need for mutual support and safety: key ingredients for survival.

Once basic survival becomes the primary need in life, self-talk messages often take on negative undertones: "The world is not a safe place"; "All conflict is bad"; "You should become passive and hope others go on their way without bothering you"; "If I attack first, I have a better chance of coming out alive"; "Don't get close to or trust anyone—you'll only be disappointed." As you move into other phases of life, these messages are unconsciously carried with you creating a self-fulfilling prophecy of low self-esteem, conflicted relationships, and an inability to achieve need fulfillment. Since you were unaware that these messages even existed, you did not even know you could confront and modify them—here's your chance!!

Remember the definition of conflict is an inability to satisfy wants and needs we *believe* are necessary for survival and happiness. Since we often mis-identify wants and needs ("What *is* the *real* problem?"), define them too broadly ("I want to be happy, I want all my problems to be solved"), or try to achieve multiple needs and wants at the same time ("Let's see, just how many balls *can* I juggle at the same time"), the results are often less than positive. This approach leaves us feeling frustrated, defensive, and confused. Whether conflict is internal (due to differences in our feelings and behavior) or involves others, unless action is taken to resolve it productively, the risk of relapse or misdirected anger skyrockets.

By the time I get to this point in my groups, my clients are saying, "Okay Jo, where's the magic dust to help us 'productively' resolve our conflicts and get some of our needs met?" My response to them *and to you* is, "There isn't any miracle cure or magic dust! Changing lifelong patterns of behavior is hard, painful work. I promise you it will hurt more before it feels better. You will be challenged by others and your own self-talk to abandon problem solving before you even learn it. Finally, the only way out is through. There are no short-cuts and no tapes to fast forward so you can skip the painful, scary parts. If you make a *firm commitment* to identify the patches on your quilt that shaped your current response choices, if you monitor and challenge negative self-talk, and if you take active steps to apply the problem-solving model presented below, things will *eventually* get better! That does *not* mean life will be perfect or that all your wants and needs will be satisfied! It means you will have a greater sense of self-control, therefore, more self-esteem. You will develop problem-solving skills to increase the likelihood of achieving long-term, *quality* sobriety. With these thoughts in mind, let's look at the problem-solving model!

The problem-solving model, whether applied to conflicts of an internal or external focus, is designed to promote honest, open communication, mutual respect, and cooperation. This model discourages labeling self or others "right or wrong" (I know this one kills you because we *all* like to be right)! The focus is on identifying and resolving the problem. After all, if somebody is injured in a football game are we going to stand there and argue about who is at fault or are we going to get help for the injured player? Although we *like* assigning blame it serves only two purposes, both of which produce destructive outcomes: It allows us to make excuses for our own inappropriate response choices ("It's *your* fault, so I don't have to change") and it allows us to feel self-righteous ("They *deserved* what they got; I *had* to drink/use/hurt myself, I *deserve* to suffer"). Another way to look at this is to ask yourself if the end justifies the means. Do two wrongs make a right (i.e., if a grocery store checker gives me too much change does that make it "right" for me to keep the money since it was not my mistake)?

The problem-solving model does not guarantee that you will achieve need fulfillment but it increases your potential of getting at least part of what you want or need. By focusing on how everyone can walk away feeling good about themselves, it provides opportunities to collectively identify potential solutions. The saying "two heads are better than one" certainly applies to this model. Even if you are attempting to resolve an internal conflict (like Jane in the earlier example) you can pull others into the problem-solving process for ideas you might not have thought about. Even when problem solving fails to produce the desired result (I get what I want) it can still be used to prevent negative consequences (I did not get what I wanted but I was able to avoid relapse and physical violence/withdrawal).

The most difficult part of the problem-solving model involves re-directing your self-talk. In order to apply the model successfully you *must* make a commitment to monitor self-talk and redirect it. If you are too confused or angry *take a time-out* to prevent yourself from falling into the trap of blaming and shaming self or others. This is very diffi-cult, especially if you are "technically" right. The ultimate goal of prob-lem solving is to successfully resolve conflict in a manner that everyone can live with. If this is not possible, the goal is to maintain control over your own behavior *regardless of what others choose to say or do.*

The problem-solving model has seven basic steps:

1. *Problem Definition.* When defining the problem, be *very* spe-cific. The biggest mistake people make is to define the problem so vaguely that it cannot be addressed. Remember Jane: "I want my prob-lems solved *now*" (a definition that provides no starting point), versus, "I want to like myself and feel like my life matters" (a specific problem with a starting point—improving Jane's self-image). Work on one prob-lem at a time and avoid the temptation to branch off into other issues while working on an identified problem (i.e., if your identified problem is how to maintain an alcohol-free status don't start working on how you can stop smoking).

2. *List ALL Possible Solutions.* Have everyone involved throw out ideas and write them down without judging them—no matter how crazy they might sound. The most challenging part about this step is the urge to judge and criticize possible solutions as they are identi-fied. When this occurs it makes people self-conscious and crushes creative ideas. This may cost you some valuable ideas/potential solu-tions. The next step allows you to think about these ideas so hold onto your opinions until all possible solutions have been identified and written down!

3. *Discuss the Potential Costs/Benefits of Each Possible Solution.* *Now* you can discuss the benefits and costs of each potential solution! Look at each option and try to realistically identify the cost to benefit ratio. If it has more potential costs than benefits, mark it off the list. If, however, it has the possibility to produce a positive outcome, leave it on your list.

4. *Choose the Best Solution or Combination of Solutions.* Once you have crossed off all possible solutions that have more negatives than positives, look at your remaining choices. Try to identify which of these options is the *best* possible solution or, if more than one has been selected, which one should be activated *first*. Remember, the goal is to find the most effective means of resolving the problem with the least amount of sacrifice for everyone involved.

5. *Develop Your Action Plan.* This step is critical to the problem-solving model. Even if you clearly identify a problem and have a first-rate solution waiting in the wings, neglecting to develop a workable action plan will sabotage even the best intentions. An action plan is to problem solving like the foundation of a house. No house will stand for long without a foundation. Likewise, successful problem resolution cannot occur in the absence of a solid action plan. When developing your action plan consider the following issues:

   a. What steps are necessary to activate this plan?
   b. Do I have the resources (time, talent, support, finances, physical endurance, emotional stability) to successfully initiate this plan?
   c. When will I put this plan into action?
   d. How will I know if my plan is working?
   e. When will I evaluate the results of my plan?

6. *Review and Praise All Efforts.* This step is also difficult because we often define success as having achieved our identified goal. In problem solving success is identified as *any attempt* to resolve a problem productively, *regardless of the outcome*! This means if I even try, I have succeeded. The first step is willingness to try new behaviors. You can always modify your plan later if you do not get the desired result on the first try. That road you traveled to get where you are is the same distance in the opposite direction. Change is a slow process so be patient and keep trying!

7. *Identify the Need for Change.* If your plan does not produce the intended results, take time to consider how you defined the problem and your action plan. Was your definition of the problem specific enough to allow for successful development of an action plan? Did you overlook anything that might have influenced the outcome? Is there something you need to add or delete to make your plan more effective? What road-blocks got in the way of your goal? After completing your review, modify the plan, and reset your target date and goals. Remember, problem solving is a *process* not a single event so keep on trying!

By now I hope you are beginning to have ideas about how the problem-solving model might work in your life. To firmly set this process in your mind, the remainder of the chapter is devoted to examples of the problem-solving process in action. Once you finish reading these examples, I invite you to use worksheet 5 and practice applying the model to areas of conflict currently occurring in your life.

EXAMPLE ONE: THE STORY OF JANE REVISITED

Earlier in this chapter I told a story about Jane, a client who wanted all her problems fixed *now*! When we left Jane, she had identified her most pressing problem as a need to like herself and feel a sense of purpose in life. Applying the problem-solving model to Jane's situation, let's pick up where we left off and see what happens!

Problem

"I want to like myself and feel like my life matters."

Jane initially identified her problem as "I want you to fix my problems and stop my emotional pain now." When encouraged to identify the *specific* problems that were causing her emotional pain Jane responded "I don't really like myself or feel like my life matters." After further discussion, Jane said she was unable to identify any positive qualities in herself. Since liking ourselves involves being able to identify and activate strengths, a good starting place for Jane is to work toward identifying at least one or two strengths. This will provide a foundation upon which she can build other pieces of her larger goal, "to like myself and feel like my life matters."

Problem Redefined

"I want to identify at least two positive qualities in myself within the next three months."

Possible Solutions

1. Get a book on self-esteem and start reading.
2. Group therapy to have peers help Jane identify her strengths.
3. Individual therapy to help Jane identify her strengths.
4. Keep drinking—then Jane doesn't have to care about liking herself.
5. Commit suicide and end the struggle.
6. Run away to Australia and start over again.
7. Find a partner and develop a sense of identity through this person.
8. Drop out of therapy and pretend "everything is fine."

Benefits and Costs of Each Possible Solution

1. Jane can always buy a book about self-esteem; however, since she doesn't believe she has any positive qualities, it is highly unlikely that reading a book will change her self-image (strike one)!
2. Group therapy sounds like a pretty good option. Jane will get support and feedback from other members and they will also confront her negative self-talk and challenge her to examine her tendency to focus on her deficiencies (let's keep this one).
3. Individual therapy is another potential option, but might work better after she has exposure to peer support and feedback: After all, the therapist *has to* say nice things about Jane! (We'll keep this as an option for later.)
4. Drinking will keep Jane comfortably numb; however, each time she sobers up she will experience guilt and shame, further damaging her self-esteem (get rid of this one fast)!
5. Suicide is certainly an option that would end the pain, but on the downside, it ends everything else too (throw this one out)!
6. Since no matter where we go, ourself goes with us, this won't help. Jane will still be depressed and lack a positive self-image whether she goes to Australia, China, or Timbuktu (discard this one).

7. Finding a partner is a great temporary distraction from the real issue—what happens when the bloom is off the rose?! (This is too good to be true, so alas, throw it out!)
8. Jane has "done that, been there!" Dropping out of therapy does not solve the problem, it increases Jane's risk of suicide, relapse, depression, and isolation (this will never do)!

Best Solution or Combination of Solutions

When we review the list of options we kept after completing the cost to benefit evaluation, we discover all but two possible solutions were discarded. Of the remaining two, the *best* solution for Jane, at least initially, appears to be group therapy. The advantages are weekly support and feedback from peers struggling with similar issues (Jane will learn she is not alone), opportunities to see how she is viewed by others, and opportunities to practice applying identified strengths at home and reporting back to the group on a weekly basis for further suggestions.

Action Plan

1. Jane will enroll in group therapy within 7 days (I had an established group so this was no problem) and commit to attending weekly sessions for at least 3 months.
2. Jane will make efforts to talk in group and to share her reactions to the feedback provided by the therapist and her peers.
3. Jane will keep a journal and record her self-talk so she can learn to identify factors that feed her negative self-image.
4. Jane will agree to ask for extra support if she has suicidal thoughts or signs of relapse.
5. Jane will review her progress weekly in group and once a month in private sessions with the therapist.

Review and Praise Efforts

By the end of the first month Jane had identified two strengths: She was kind to others and she was intelligent. She admitted that although she knew these things were true, she had to work very hard to avoid letting negative self-talk undo these strengths. By the end of the second month, Jane had identified two more strengths: She was courageous (willing to attempt change), and she kept her commitments. She said it was a little easier to accept praise from others, but she still tended to focus on weaknesses, especially when depressed. By the end of the third month, Jane had identified six strengths, maintained her sobriety, and was finding it easier to identify times when she was most vulnerable to negative self-talk (thanks to her faithful journal keeping). Jane was clearly uncomfortable when the group praised all her hard work and the progress she had made, but she was able to stay in the session and share her discomfort out loud with other group members.

Problem Areas for Additional Action

1. Jane had made good progress; however, her new thoughts and behavior were only in their infancy. Her action plan was modified to extend her stay in group for another three months.
2. A second change included weekly individual therapy sessions to help Jane identify ways to work better in group.

Jane's conflict is clearly internally focused. Indeed, Jane is her own worst enemy. Her negative self-talk creates a self-destructive cycle of shame, blame, depression with suicidal thoughts, and relapse. As demonstrated in the example above, problem solving works well with self-directed conflict. Internal conflict undermines need fulfillment (Jane's lack of a positive self-image prevented her from experiencing pleasure in daily life). If you are a person, like Jane, whose internal conflicts keep you from finding the happiness you deserve, the problem-solving model provides options for confronting and modifying self-defeating patterns of thinking and behaving. It is equally effective in resolving conflict arising from outside sources. Let's look at another example.

EXAMPLE TWO: IF YOU MOW IT, YOU BLOW IT

My neighbors hire a lawn service to provide upkeep on their lawn. Unfortunately, when the workers mow and edge, they leave grass and leaves strewn up and down my driveway. This example demonstrates the use of problem solving when others are involved *and* willing to work on problems together.

Problem

"My neighbors' lawn service leaves a mess on my driveway that I have to clean up."

Possible Solutions

1. Move to another neighborhood.
2. Talk to my neighbors about the problem and ask them to correct it.
3. Talk to the workers directly and express my concerns.
4. Set a trap and ambush the workers when I catch them leaving a mess behind.
5. Yell at and threaten the workers when they leave a mess behind.
6. Poison the neighbors' grass so it all dies and then there's no reason for them to hire a lawn service.
7. Continue to clean up the mess and say nothing.
8. Blow leaves and grass on the neighbors' walks and street when I mow and edge our lawn.

Benefits and Costs of Each Possible Solution

1. Like nobody else uses lawn services! Besides, I like my house and don't want to move (cross it off).
2. A possibility if I cannot resolve the problem directly with the workers (keep this one as a possible option).
3. Gee, what a novel idea! Start at the source and proceed accordingly (definitely a keeper).
4. Sounds rather excessive, doesn't it? Besides, if I get aggressive, I might end up in jail and I'll *still* have the mess to contend with when I get home (definitely put this one in file 13).
5. Great! Then all my neighbors can say, "Did you see Jo go ballistic? If she's a mental health professional, I fear for the safety of her clients!" (It's not worth it, throw this one out fast.)

6. I hardly think I can afford to resod my neighbors' lawn if I get caught. Even if they never catch me, I couldn't live with the guilt of doing something so underhanded. I know how much stress that would cause for my neighbors and they're really nice people (throw this one out).

7. Remember in chapter 7 when we talked about passive–explosive behavior? Well, keeping quiet is a setup for a future explosion (not even an option).

8. Seems pretty childish to me and eventually they'll catch on and think I'm nuts. After all, if I never tell them *why* I'm doing it, they won't make the connection between what their lawn service does to my driveway and what I am doing to theirs (no, no, a thousand times no)!

Best Solution or Combination of Solutions

Well, we certainly shot down most of our options, but wasn't it fun? We have two remaining options that look pretty good: Talk directly to the workers, and if this fails, talk to my neighbors.

Action Plan

1. I decided to approach the workers with my concerns within one week of the last episode of "mess making" (they come on a weekly basis and luckily, their scheduled day of service is on my day off).

2. I thought about what I needed to say and developed an "I message" so my comments could be made without blaming or shaming.

3. The following week, when the workers had completed their lawn work, and were preparing to leave without sweeping my walk, I approached the lead worker.

4. I stated, "When you mow my neighbors' lawn and leave grass and leaves on my driveway I feel frustrated because it makes extra work for me. I would really appreciate it if you would make an effort to clean up the mess on my driveway before you leave."

5. The worker's initial response was to say, "I don't think *we* do that."

6. My next response was, "I would appreciate it if you would come with me for a minute so I can show you what I am talking about."

7. I showed him the area and he agreed they had indeed left a mess and would take more care in the future to leave my driveway in better shape.

8. I monitored the situation for several weeks and they kept to their commitment to sweep or blow grass and leaves off my driveway when they made a mess.

9. This incident occurred a year ago and I rarely see "unacceptable" amounts of grass or leaves on my driveway.

Review and Praise Efforts

Ten years ago I would have "stuffed" my anger and later probably yelled at the workers for being so irresponsible. I patted myself on the back for redirecting my self-talk and using time-out and problem solving to identify a *reasonable* plan for resolving this issue. I was able to resolve the conflict productively so felt good about myself, avoided conflict with my neighbors, and treated the workers with the respect they deserved (after all, how can you be mad at someone if you don't tell them that you are angry and give them an opportunity to modify their behavior)?

Problem Areas for Additional Action

None.

I know, I can hear you now: "Jo, not everyone is so cooperative as those lawn men were! What do you do when you have a conflict and the other person either refuses to cooperate or becomes hostile and defensive toward you?" This is a very valid question! In the "ideal world" we identified at the beginning of this chapter, problem solving would generate the desired result every time. Alas, in the real world things are not so easy. When you are confronted with situations that involve others who are clearly unwilling or unable to participate in problem solving, the goal becomes damage containment. Yes, you may be "right" and the other person may really be a jackass, *but* is it worth losing your sobriety and/or misdirecting your anger so *you* become a jackass to prove your point? Carefully consider the long-term costs of those few minutes of pleasure you get from becoming aggressive or activating your addiction. It may cost more than it's worth! As I have stated throughout this book *I can't make you* change! You can choose whatever response you feel compelled to activate. I will respect your choice; however, I will also hold you accountable for your actions and their consequence, and so will the rest of the world! Let's look at one final example to help you see why you *might* want to redirect self-defeating thoughts, apply time-out, and engage the problem-solving model to reduce your negative consequences—even when that SOB *deserves* to suffer!

EXAMPLE THREE: THE EX-WIFE FROM HELL

Problem

"My ex-wife is verbally abusive when I pick up my children for visitation and is unwilling to stop this behavior."

Possible Solutions

1. Kill the ***###@@ and put an end to it once and for all.
2. Catch the ***###@@ alone and "hurt her a little" so she gets the message.
3. Become verbally abusive back to her (after all, *she* started it)!
4. Ignore her and hope she finally stops being so childish.
5. Call Child Protective Services and have the children taken away from her since she's "crazy."
6. Have someone go with me to pick up the kids.
7. Have someone else pick up the kids.
8. Petition the court for custody of the children.
9. Stop seeing my kids until they are big enough to come to me on their own.

Benefits and Cost of Each Possible Solution

1. "What an adrenaline high! It would feel *sooo* good to terminate that problem, *but*, then my children would be motherless,

they would be traumatized by the violent nature of their mother's death, if I get caught I will go to prison (or the gas chamber) and never see my children again" (throw it out quick before it's too late).

2. "Same problem as number one, it will cause harm to my children and since she's not dead, she will probably see to it I *never* see my kids again" (throw it out).

3. "Yeah, right! This might feel pretty good but what will my kids think when they see their parents screaming and yelling in the street? Two rights don't make a wrong!" (throw it out).

4. "Might work, after all, it's only been a month since the divorce" (keep it as a potential option).

5. "Turn about is fair play, she could call them on me too and then where will the kids be! Besides, if Child Protective Services gets involved no telling what could happen" (this is too weird to even consider).

6. "Hey, another possibility! If this person is uninvolved, even if she becomes verbally abusive, they can help me remember why I should avoid playing into this game" (worth considering).

7. "Have someone else pick up the kids for me. Well, great idea but she already said she will not deliver them to anyone but me unless a court order forces her to. Pretty extreme but I don't want to start a power struggle" (put this one in file 12 just in case I need it later).

8. "This is certainly an option, but it is costly and will take time, what do I do in the meantime?" (not a solution to the immediate problem).

9. "*Not!* My kids are only 5 and 7, they would forget me before they are old enough to drive" (toss this one).

Best Solution or Combination of Solutions

Since my client had much to lose by becoming violent, feeding into his ex-partner's rage, or abandoning his children, numbers 1, 2, 3, 5, 7, and 9 are out. Although a long-range possibility, number 8 will not solve the immediate problem, so it too is set aside. At this point, numbers 4 and 6 appear to be the most *productive* alternatives: Working hard to avoid playing into this power struggle and taking along a support person as a reality check.

Action Plan

1. Before the next scheduled visitation (which was one week away) the client would practice applying time-out and detouring self-talk to help prepare him for the expected verbal assaults from his ex-spouse (this was accomplished in group role-plays where I played a hostile, aggressive spouse and he practiced both ignoring my responses and maintaining very calm, short responses when replies were unavoidable).

2. Before the next scheduled visitation, my client was to contact a friend who could go along for support and reality testing (this was accomplished).

3. My client was to keep a journal to record destructive self-talk when he thought about his ex-spouse and develop statements to redirect these thoughts (i.e., "She's just upset, why take it personally; how embarrassing for her to be so out of control; nothing lasts forever, eventually she'll get tired of this game; if I don't feed into this behavior my children will be less upset"). These were identified in group and used during role-play sessions.

4. My client agreed to apply this plan for 3 months (six contacts with his ex-spouse). If by that time no change was noted, he would pursue the advice of his lawyer.

Review and Praise All Efforts

My client continued to pick up his children for regularly scheduled times of visitation. He took his friend along on these visits and was able to refrain from becoming verbally or physically abusive although he certainly thought about it! Although his spouse continued her verbal assaults, over time he developed an ability to "tune her out" and take it less personally. After several months, her behavior, though still inappropriate at times, was less extreme. He was praised by the leader and group members for his efforts and encouraged to keep up the good work.

Problem Areas for Additional Action

After the first two visits following the development of his action plan, my client expressed concern regarding how his wife's behavior was affecting his children. They were always upset and tearful when switching homes since she became verbally abusive toward my client on sight. Since he could not control her behavior, the group helped him problem solve the issue further. The consensus was that he should explain to his children that their mother was just very upset about the divorce. He would avoid judging and blaming her and then discharge his anger in group or with his friend to reduce the risk of a passive–explosive reaction or relapse. He also encouraged the children to let him know if they needed to talk about their feelings once they got to his house. He initiated this action at the next visit and it seemed to reduce the children's anxiety and confusion.

No additional action was identified at the point of this client's last contact with this therapist.

I'm sure some of you had very strong, negative reactions when you read the above example! My client was in a very tough spot but needed to use his anger management skills to contain his own aggressive urges since his ex-partner could not and he had to see her in order to assume custody of his children. The use of time-out, detouring self-talk, and problem solving were vital to his effective redirection of anger and maintenance of sobriety. As I stated earlier, sometimes we find ourselves in situations where we really are "*right!*" Where the other person's behavior is *so* inappropriate that they deserve whatever they get. And yes, you can become aggressive or use these events to justify a relapse, but at whose expense? *Before* selecting a response choice, respect yourself enough to take a time-out and *think* constructively about the potential benefits and costs of your actions. At least then, you can make a decision *knowing* the consequences that await you.

I hope this chapter has challenged your thinking and given you ideas about how you might change your own behavior regardless of how others respond. The goal is to maximize your potential for positive outcomes (need fulfillment) and minimize your potential for negative consequences. After all, the only person we *really* have control over is ourselves. One last example to help you understand the importance of problem solving.

If you were planning to buy a new car would you pick a car with standard or antilock brakes? Would you choose a car with or without airbags and seat belts? Would you want that car to have working lights, an audible horn, and safety flashers? Most of us would answer all these questions by saying, "I want a car that has as many safety features as possible to increase my potential for arriving safely at my destination." If you wouldn't drive a car without safety features, how can you possibly think of going through daily life without having and applying anger management relapse prevention skills? After all, we can always buy a new car, we only have one of ourselves! Think about this every time you want to return to old, self-destructive patterns of behavior—don't you think you deserve all the safety features you can learn and apply? If you are ready to try your hand at problem solving turn to Worksheet 4.

WORKSHEET 4

<u>USING THE PROBLEM-SOLVING MODEL</u>

This worksheet is designed to help you begin the process of identifying and resolving conflicts that arise from unmet needs. Whether this conflict is an inside job or involves other people, the problem-solving model provides options to increase your chances of a positive outcome. (Remember this not only means getting what you want and need, it also means avoiding negative consequences regardless of what others say or do.) Using the examples provided in chapter 8, complete this worksheet (remember to use a new page for each individual problem) and see how creatively you can apply this model to real life issues. *Good Luck!*

1. The Problem: _____

_____

2. Possible Solutions (Remember not to judge them yet!):

A. _____

B. _____

C _____

D. _____

E. _____

F. _____

3. Benefits and Costs of Each Potential Solution:

A. _____

B. _____

C _____

D. _____
E. _____
F. _____

4. Best Solution or Combination of Solutions:

A. _____
B. _____
C _____
D. _____

5. Action Plan:

A. _____
B. _____
C _____
D. _____
E. _____

6. Review and Praise All Efforts: _____
_____
_____

7. Problem Areas for Additional Action:

A. _____
B. _____
C _____
D. _____

9

Balancing Your Boundaries

When I was a child *Lost in Space* was a popular television series. The main characters were the Robinson family, their robot, and Dr. Smith, a rather anxious fellow whose overactive imagination led to some interesting experiences! The Robinsons were space travelers who had lost their way. Each episode involved encounters with alien life forms and the Robinsons' struggle to stay alive. One of their defenses was the robot who shouted, "Warning! warning! danger! danger" when it sensed dangerous aliens nearby. A second safeguard was a force field that stopped anything trying to approach their spaceship.

Unfortunately, the slightest hint of danger triggered Dr. Smith to turn on the force field. When scolded for his childlike reactions, he defended his behavior by stating, "Better safe than sorry!" Dr. Smith's distorted beliefs about danger (remember the patches on your quilt and how they can create distorted beliefs about life events) often created more problems than they solved. Family members were frequently placed in high-risk situations because Dr. Smith turned on the force field before checking to see if the Robinsons were safely within its borders. At other times, potential sources of friendship and help were foiled by his reckless overreactions. The moral of this story: You have to learn when to turn your force field on and off! Neglecting this important detail (by over- or underreacting) seriously undermines any potential benefits this safeguard might provide.

By now you are probably thinking, "So what does this have to do with anger management and relapse prevention?" Take out worksheets 1 and 2 where you identified how life experiences shaped and continue to influence factors that trigger your reactions (physical, emotional, cognitive, and behavioral cues). Learning how and when to activate and deactivate defense mechanisms (response choices) requires us to recognize distortions in self-talk messages created by life experiences. The following questions are helpful in accomplishing this task: "How, when, and where did I learn what I came to identify as the truth about events in my life?" "Why do I accept and continue to replay these messages even after repeatedly experiencing negative consequences?" "Is it too late to challenge distorted messages and replace them with a more accurate set of beliefs?" Until long-standing patterns of thinking and behaving are identified and challenged, your response choices will be guided by distorted, and often self-destructive, messages. To this end, your ability to identify and set in motion realistic boundaries for yourself (what you will/won't, can/cannot do and what you want/don't want) will be dangerously impaired.

Applying this idea to the anger–relapse cycle we discover repeated episodes of relapse occur when individuals lack the ability to set realistic boundaries for themselves. If I cannot identify the driving forces behind my wants and needs, and develop methods to promote their satisfaction (or redefine them more realistically), my risk of misdirected anger and relapse becomes enormous. Likewise, if I cannot identify the point at which I need to establish realistic limits (say no when to say yes would place me at risk of compromising my physical and/or emotional well-being), and the factors that drive me to overextend despite clear warning signs of danger, my risk of misdirected anger and relapse is equally great. Let's look at an example of this process in action.

Jan (not her real name) was raised in an Irish-American family that upheld traditions of the old country. One of these traditions was the use of alcohol to encourage closeness and communication between family members. Drinking alcoholic beverages was seen as a "normal" part of daily life. Even when a family member overdid it, the typical response was "Oh my, it looks like _____ had a wee bit too much to drink— let's see that he or she gets safely tucked into bed." Growing up in this environment, Jan "learned" that using alcohol on a daily basis was not only acceptable but normal. This distorted view of drinking shaped Jan's beliefs about alcohol use and its role in her life.

This process of learning that alcohol use is "normal" was passed on nonverbally and modeled by older family members. Jan's self-talk was an *unconscious product* of family patterns of alcohol use that she never questioned (remember the story about the family that always cut both ends off the ham before cooking it without asking why). The patches on her quilt supported the belief that daily alcohol use was "normal." When she was no longer able to drink without experiencing negative consequences (depression and stomach problems) Jan thought *she* was somehow to blame. When Jan tried to stop drinking she had difficulty telling family members no when a drink was offered. Her reluctance was based on "learned" messages that a drink is a sign of respect and friendship, and, therefore, should *never* be refused.

A second factor that made it difficult for Jan to say no was her belief that saying no would somehow "mark" her as different and unacceptable. Asking for family support was equally difficult because giving up alcohol represented a significant loss to members of her culture. To further complicate matters, Jan not only faced the challenge of confronting long-standing cultural and family beliefs, she also unconsciously struggled with the unspoken rules so common in chemically dependent families (don't talk, trust, or feel).

Jan's first task was to understand how cultural beliefs and family values shaped and continued to influence her views about alcohol. This process was essential to sobriety since giving up alcohol seriously challenged her belief system. Achieving this goal required Jan to identify the content of self-talk messages and determine the connection between these messages and her family and cultural background. Distortions in her thinking (if you don't drink, something is wrong with you) created guilt and anxiety whenever she attempted to stop drinking. Once this process was identified Jan challenged and redirected thoughts that increased her potential for relapse. Accomplishing this task required Jan to adjust her beliefs so neither she nor her family and cultural beliefs were wrong. The daily use of alcohol was simply no longer a realistic option given her individual needs and circumstances. Jan offset the loss of alcohol by challenging the belief that alcohol was critical to individual and family well-being. She replaced it with the belief that sobriety, to prevent further physical and mental decline, was vital to her long-term survival—*regardless of others' reactions*. This required considerable support from her therapist and group members since Jan was attempting to change beliefs she had upheld for over 40 years.

As we saw in the above example, distortions in thinking and behavior often occur without our conscious awareness. We move through life following set patterns of behavior, never stopping to think "does what I believed at 5, 15, 25, still apply in the here-and-now?" This lack of understanding prevents us from challenging and redirecting our response choices—until someone or something questions their validity. Let's look at another example, this time using a physical disability.

My youngest son was born 13 weeks prematurely and medical interventions necessary to save his life destroyed most of his vision. Since this happened during infancy, he never experienced normal vision. His understanding of "normal" is what *he* sees (i.e., he thinks everyone's picture of the world matches his own). My son's visual impairment seriously affects his ability to judge height and distance. When navigating stairs, curbs, or other uneven surfaces, he bends down and feels his way. This behavior, although "odd" to unsuspecting onlookers, is "normal" for him. At age 3 he is unaware of what others think about his behavior so never questions it (this is starting to sound a lot like the first example, isn't it)? As he grows up, his awareness of others' reactions will become sharper. Once aware, he will need to develop a belief system that supports his behavior (action he takes to judge height and distance) are necessary for successful participation in the world. Recognizing this fact will help him develop *realistic boundaries* to avoid creating set-ups for failure (i.e., acting "as if" he were fully sighted)!

Developing awareness of how and why we think and behave as we do is critical to effective boundary setting. To accomplish this task we must identify and offset distortions in our belief system. This means challenging beliefs about *what was, what might have been, what is, what can never be, and what might be* so an acceptable balance between our thoughts and behavior can develop. For a chemically dependent individual this means challenging the belief that substance abuse is the only way to cope with painful life events or "fit in" with family members and friends. When cultural values are involved, as shown in Jan's story, the goal is to consider whether current beliefs still "fit" *for that individual*. Individuals with physical or mental disorders must come to terms with the reality that former patterns of behavior may no longer be possible (i.e., if I break my neck I can no longer participate in track meets; if I have an emotional illness, I may lack the ability to perform tasks I formerly excelled at). For those who implode or explore anger it means identifying feelings behind their anger mask. Until we understand *the meaning* behind current thoughts and behavior, and develop acceptable ways to redefine existing beliefs, realistic boundaries cannot be established.

This difficult process requires us to examine factors that shaped and continue to influence our response choices. Six factors, stemming from life experiences and the beliefs they give rise to, are critical for individuals with misdirected anger and substance abuse issues:

1. *We fear rejection.* If life experiences "teach" me that asking for what I want only leads to disappointment, and saying no sets me up for ridicule, abuse, or neglect, I "learn" to hide my true feelings. This creates the belief that no matter how much I want something I should *never* ask because I will only be disappointed and no matter how desperately I want to say no, if I do there will be dreadful consequences. Although these beliefs may be true during certain periods of my life (as a small child being sexually, emotionally, or physically abused) as I move into different phases of life and develop new relationships, I unconsciously carry these beliefs with me. Since I believe they are "true for life," I never challenge them in the here-and-now. The results: a self-fulfilling prophecy of unmet needs, relationship conflicts, relapse, and poor self-esteem.

2. *The issue of commitment.* If past experience taught me that "promises are made to be broken," it becomes almost impossible to believe that others might *really* follow through if I ask for what I want and need. Likewise, if *my own* past behavior has been undependable, I may resist making commitments to avoid the risk of not living up to them. The issue of commitment also interferes with my ability to set limits (say no) when I either cannot or do not want to satisfy the requests of others. If I have abandoned/been abandoned, or punished/been punished for saying no in my past, I will *unconsciously* avoid recreating this experience regardless of the cost (relapse, misdirected anger, poor self-esteem).

3. *All or none thinking.* As we go through life, "set" ways of thinking and behaving arise. Much like the mule that methodically plods round and round on the "Flying Jenny" ride at carnivals, we unconsciously "learn" to think and act in certain ways. As time passes, these patterns of thinking and behaving (realistic or not) become our reality. Even when the mule is not harnessed to the Flying Jenny it continues walking in circles. Rare is the day a mule steps outside the rut it has created to explore alternative paths. Unfortunately, people become as conditioned as mules when it comes to thoughts and behavior!

All or none thinking, when applied to boundary setting, creates *big* trouble. If it's "my way or the highway," right or wrong, good or bad then *somebody* has to be wrong (and it's not me). With all or none thinking if we can't have it all, we don't want anything. Since this belief system develops across time, we fail to identify the connection between our actions and their consequences. The result: misdirected anger, social isolation, poor self-esteem (there *must* be something wrong with me *even though I'm right* because people are always mad at me), and relapse.

4. *We feel obliged to respond IMMEDIATELY.* This urgency to provide instant responses to others' requests is directly linked to our need for acceptance. This is especially true for individuals with substance abuse disorders since addiction creates a series of losses (shattered relationships, employment, financial crisis, legal consequences, declining health) that negatively affect self-image. The resulting shame and self-directed blame set us up to make unrealistic promises (saying yes when we need to say no). These promises, made impulsively, arise with little thought of whether we can successfully manage another responsibility without hurting ourselves. This increases the risk of failure (saying yes and being unable to meet *all* my commitments), misdirected anger, and relapse.

5. *We believe a LOGICAL explanation for our response MUST ALWAYS exist.* Although we would like to believe that everything we want is possible if only we would ask, realistically, we expect some negative responses. Since we "know" nobody gets everything they ask for, *why* do we believe others think *we* will always meet *their* needs? To answer this question, take a look at the patches on your quilt! If past experiences involved people with unrealistic demands, you "learned" that honoring *all* requests (or having a very good reason why you couldn't) was vital to avoid negative consequences. As you grew up, these beliefs were never challenged (you never knew that you could/ should). This unconscious process creates a great sense of urgency to provide immediate, detailed, and believable explanations for all "no" responses. We never consider that people *expect* some no's in life (I do, don't you?)! We also lose sight of the fact that when we do say no, most people prefer a simple yes or no not some marathon excuse that takes 15 minutes! The need to provide a suitable answer for saying no is especially urgent if others experienced pain or embarrassment as a result of our misdirected anger or substance abuse. The tension arising from the need to *explain, explain, explain* generates resentment, misdirected anger, and relapse!

  6. *We are afraid of what others will think about us.* How often do you spend large amounts of time and energy questioning the whys and wherefores when someone asks you for something they need or says no when you request something from them? The usual thought is, "They must have a good reason for asking or saying no." Unless the other person is *always* asking or *always* saying no, little energy goes into judging their responses. Since we allow others the luxury of asking and saying no without attaching negative labels to them, why do we assume negative labels will be attached to us if *we* ask or say no!?

  A review of past behavior (especially during periods of active substance abuse) helps answer this question. If you *repeatedly* asked for support while drinking or using drugs others may have labeled you a user, manipulator, bum, leech. If your addiction exposed you to exploitation (always saying yes so you could get your next fix) you may have been labeled easy, a mark, soft, a pushover. While these labels might have applied during periods of active addiction, you "forgot" to challenge them once you became sober.

  Neglecting to challenge whether negative labels apply to *current* behavior is a setup for unmet needs and/or overextension! Poor self-esteem resulting from past behavior, and prejudices held by those who remember your behavior during active addiction, foster the tendency to "buy into" negative labels even when they no longer apply. This is why participation in a substance abuse treatment program, with your family if possible, is so important! Redirecting the self-defeating thoughts and behavior created by negative labels is painful but *must* occur or you will lack the courage to set realistic boundaries critical to long-term, quality sobriety.

  So, with all these odds stacked against you, is change *really* possible? Well, that all depends on you. If you allow the past to govern your present, you will blame others when feeling needy or overwhelmed. This prevents any possibility of achieving the self-awareness necessary to create a sober life-style. If, on the other hand, you take responsibility for setting boundaries you can live with, the possibility of achieving long-term, quality sobriety is high. Yes, you're right, there is a catch: You have to be willing to accept *personal responsibility* for making things happen in your life! This means taking the bull by the horns, facing the music, charging full-speed ahead, and taking risks you never thought you were capable of taking.

The notion of personal responsibility ties in beautifully with step 4: making a fearless and searching inventory of ourselves. The transition from perceiving ourselves as "victims of circumstance" to "guiding forces of our own destiny" is the first step in this process. Past experience must be viewed as a teaching tool rather than an excuse for further substance abuse. We cannot change the past, no matter how hard we try, but we *can* learn from it and use this knowledge to reduce the risk of repeating similar mistakes in the present and future. Learning to set realistic boundaries, and adjust them as life circumstances change, is essential to recovery.

Where to begin? As I have stated throughout this chapter, and indeed the entire book, recognizing how and why you came to think and behave as you do is the first step in creating shifts in response choices. Understanding the forces that drive current patterns of thinking and behaving prepares you to challenge and replace distorted beliefs with more realistic options. The next step involves learning to ask for what you want and to say no productively (see Worksheet 5, pp. 121–124). Let's look at some examples so you can see how this process works in "the real world."

EXAMPLE ONE: I WANT TO WRITE

My passion in life is writing. I often imagine what it would be like if I had the time and money to retreat to the woods and spend my time writing, walking, and riding horses. Unfortunately, like most of you, I have commitments that prevent this fantasy from becoming a reality (at least for now). My first task in developing realistic boundaries was to think about why this need is so important at this point in my life (why this, why now). As I said earlier, I am rapidly approaching midlife and want to make a difference in this world before passing on to the next. Writing is one path I have chosen to achieve this goal.

If I hold onto the unrealistic belief that I must devote my entire life to writing, I would abandon my family and career. By defining my needs and beliefs to accommodate *current* commitments (a husband, children, active career, friendships), I identified what I needed to ask for and say no to in order to accomplish my goal. What I need most is time, so I reviewed my schedule to see how I might carve out blocks of time for uninterrupted writing. Sunday seemed to be the perfect option, with one catch—I have a 3-year-old son! I approached my husband and identified my need, and the reasons behind it. Since he loves me very much, he agreed to devote his time on Sundays to our son so I would be free to write.

A second need was a quiet place to write since my active family keeps our house hopping! I decided that my office is ideal since no one is at the clinic on weekends. I can spend 10 or 12 hours writing without interruptions, then go home and spend the remainder of my time meeting family- and career-related needs. I also had to redefine my workload. Since one day was devoted to writing, that meant one day less to accomplish household tasks and participate in family activities. I put several things on hold and alerted family members and friends of my plan so they would understand my lack of availability. I also set aside several weekends up front as "family weekends" during which I would forego my writing activities (one was to take a family trip to our property in Palestine, Texas, a second to accommodate my grandmother's 90th birthday party, and a third to participate in a family vacation). I also lowered my standards for keeping a spotless house and creative meals on the table.

As you can see, effective boundary setting takes quite a bit of thought and planning! I can say from my own experience that putting forth the effort to identify and establish boundaries during different phases of your life will create positive feelings about yourself and the events in your life. Boundary setting allowed me to "have it all." I can keep my family, my career, and *still* write! Had I *not* taken the time to identify and activate boundaries to fit this phase in my life, you would not be reading this book!

Ah yes, there are several little glitches in this approach! You have to be honest with yourself and others, risk sharing what you think and feel out loud, accept some no's, and creatively develop alternative plans (if plan A doesn't work what about plans B, C, D?). You have to accept *personal responsibility* for making things happen, or not happen. It's also up to you to change your plan when things don't work out as you had initially predicted. I know it is hard to believe, but these risks are worth it! Remember, the biggest risk in life is to risk nothing. If you never take a risk, you will never change and the uncomfortable but familiar rut that keeps you stuck in self-destructive patterns of behavior will continue. Let's look at a second example demonstrating the potential benefits of boundary setting.

EXAMPLE TWO: IS IT TOO LATE TO REBUILD MY LIFE?

Susan (not her real name) dropped out of high school in her senior year to get married. She was *sure* that once she "escaped" from home and the demands of high school life would be wonderful (no rules, you can do whatever you want). Much to her dismay, what she discovered was that without education she was doomed to a minimum wage job. The lack of maturity in both herself and her partner also created relationship conflicts that led to emotional and verbal abuse. As time passed Susan felt more and more powerless to change her life. Her husband frequently told her she was stupid and ugly, that nobody would ever love her the way *he* did. After the birth of her daughter, the emotional and verbal abuse increased because Susan's husband was jealous of the attention she devoted to the baby. Susan was ashamed and embarrassed about the mess she had made of her life so she kept her misery to herself. This self-imposed isolation made it difficult for Susan to test out her beliefs about herself and her situation. She eventually began to believe she *was* stupid and unattractive.

Susan stayed trapped in this self-destructive relationship for more than ten years. Too fearful to ask for help, she believed she was doomed to a life of misery and abuse. The turning point for Susan was when her daughter developed emotional problems related to their abusive home situation. She realized that for the sake of her child, she *must* act. Susan's boundaries had been badly eroded over time. She had no self-confidence, believed herself to be stupid and ugly, and had no idea about how to begin the process of rebuilding her life. Her only close friend unknowingly provided the catalyst for change when she said, "Susan, I hope someday you see yourself as I do, you are such a wonderful human being." This statement prompted Susan to seek therapy since she knew she could not change on her own.

The therapist's first goal was to help Susan identify self-defeating beliefs about herself and her life circumstances. Her sense of self was so distorted she could not identify any personal strengths or decide what to do with the rest of her life. The therapist helped Susan identify negative messages she received about herself both during childhood and marriage. Gradually, she learned to challenge self-defeating thoughts and replace them with more productive alternatives. The belief "I am stupid, ugly, and nobody will want me" was replaced with "I have intelligence, I am attractive, and I have a lot to contribute to others." Group therapy was also helpful since her peers refused to accept her negative descriptions of herself. They gently but firmly pointed out self-destructive responses when Susan returned to old patterns of behavior in group.

To successfully complete the boundary-setting process Susan took the following steps:

1. Individual and group therapy to identify self-destructive patterns of thinking and behavior and replace them with positive alternatives.
2. Family therapy so she and her daughter could mend the wounds created by years of family conflict (Susan divorced her husband after a year of therapy).
3. Career counseling to help Susan identify job opportunities.
4. Increasing her support network (Susan reconnected with family and friends and developed new friendships and outside interests) to create a more balanced life-style.

As with the first example, this required a great deal of time, energy, and commitment on Susan's part. She was often afraid and stated she would have quit on many occasions had it not been for the support of her friend and the needs of her child. Susan was forced to confront her worst fears about herself ("I am stupid, ugly, nobody else will want me"). This was especially frightening because she was afraid these beliefs were true! The more she confronted her irrational beliefs, and surrounded herself with family and friends who focused on her strengths, the easier it became to consider the possibility that she might indeed have better things in store.

Over the course of a year, Susan developed a beginning core of self-esteem. She started taking college courses part-time, and expanded her social supports. When she left therapy she could not believe how far she had come, and realized she had much work yet to do on creating and maintaining boundaries she could live with. One of her biggest sources of motivation was to remember where she started and how, without that first step toward treatment (as frightening as it had been), she would still be unhappily married, with the belief that her life could never change.

WORKSHEET 5

GUIDELINES: ASKING FOR WHAT YOU WANT/LEARNING TO SAY NO

Asking for what you want and saying no require patience and practice. The following guidelines will increase your ability to set boundaries that you, and those you love, can live with. After reviewing the guidelines, complete the practice exercise keeping the following thoughts in mind:

1. Which of the six factors identified as roadblocks to effective boundary setting interfere with *your* ability to ask for what you want and say no?

2. Are there certain people in your life that you have more difficulty setting boundaries with than others? What beliefs discourage you from applying boundary setting strategies with them?

Asking for what you want:

1. State your request calmly and directly:

   "I would like _____"

   "I want or need _____"

2. Avoid language that is demanding or hostile:

   "You have to"   "You should"   "If you don't _____ I'll . . ."

   "I expect . . ."   "This is how it is"   "You must do what I want"

Worksheet 5 (continued)

3. Be prepared to receive some no's. Remember, nobody *always* gets what they want and others have the same right to say no that you do! If the other person is honest enough to say no, at least you know where you stand and can explore other options.

Nondefensive strategies for saying no:

1. Clearly and calmly state your response, "No, I can't _____."

2. If you provide an explanation, keep it short and simple!

   Like this: "No, I can't baby-sit this weekend, I have other plans."

   NOT this: "Gee, I wish you would have called sooner. I have to take Sam for a haircut, then there's the brownie meeting I promised to take Sarah to, and I have to write up a proposal for work this weekend. I really would love to help but things are really hectic right now—sorry!"

3. When declining requests, present your answer calmly. Remember, you have the right to say no. There is no need to get defensive (if you do, look at past experiences and see *why* you feel so threatened)!

4. If the other person refuses to accept no for an answer do not feel obligated to argue your position. Remember, the goal is to respond (YES or NO) and maintain control of your own behavior *regardless of the other person's response!* If you are at risk of misdirecting *your* anger, take a time-out. It's better to remove yourself from an unpleasant situation than to create negative consequences that could have been avoided (relationship conflicts, relapse).

ASKING FOR WHAT YOU WANT/SAYING NO

PRACTICE EXERCISE

1. Identify a person you *repeatedly* have difficulty asking for what you want from or saying no to (who is this person and how are you related: friend, coworker, family member.)

   _____

   _____

2. What factors prevent you from setting realistic boundaries with this person?

   _____

   _____

3. What past experiences have you had with this person that support your belief that it is pointless to ask for what you want or say no?

   _____

   _____

4. Using the guidelines presented above, what do you want or need from this person and how can you productively identify this need?

   _____

   _____

   _____

5. If they decline your request, what alternatives do you have for satisfying your need?

   _____

   _____

   _____

Worksheet 5 (continued)

6. What request has this person made that you wish you had declined?

7. What led you to say yes when you wanted to say no?

8. Using the guidelines presented above, how can you productively decline requests in the future?

9. If the person has a negative reaction to your request or decline, what steps can be taken to productively redirect *your responses?*

FINAL SUGGESTIONS

Use this exercise on a regular basis to practice boundary setting with people at home, work, play, in public places with strangers. Some will cooperate and be delighted that you are making efforts to communicate productively. Those who feel threatened will consciously and unconsciously attempt to sabotage your best efforts. As your skills increase, you will get better at recognizing that although responses may *feel/very* personal, they are *really* statements about how the other person is feeling—you just happen to be in their flight path! Remember: *Your* goal is long-term, quality sobriety. To achieve this goal, you *must* identify and activate boundaries *that work for you.*

10

The Elastic in Your Underwear

Most of us don't give much thought to our underwear. We get up, shower, get dressed, and go about our day. We rarely pay much attention to those special instructions on the label (cold water wash only, hang to dry, avoid bleach). Do manufacturers *really* think we have time to read the labels, much less follow the instructions!? I'm as guilty as everyone else when it comes to throwing a pair of panties or a bra into the gaping jaws of a washer loaded with heavy denim, bleach, and *hot water*! Life is just too short to read labels—isn't it? Let's hope by the end of this chapter you'll rethink that one.

The only time we notice our underwear is when it gets really old and the elastic breaks down. When it starts falling down around our ankles (or bra straps get so frayed they slide down our shoulders). *Then*, we *finally* realize the *true significance* of underwear! Once we finally notice our underwear has reached the point of no return, it's off to the store on our lunch hour to buy more so we can start the whole process over again.

Well folks, we pay just about as much attention to our state of emotional well-being as we do to our underwear. That is, *until* we experience relapse or an episode of misdirected anger! Now those things *get our attention*! We take it for granted that we have an unlimited credit line for navigating life stresses. Rarely do we consider whether we are pulsing out more emotional energy than is currently in reserve. Unfortunately, our minds don't work like the teller machine at your bank. Teller machines have built-in safety features to prevent overdrafts. If you ask for more money than is available, instead of cash, you get one of those little slips that says "insufficient funds to complete this transaction." Although annoying, it sure saves time and embarrassment down the road. When we overdraw emotionally, consequences can be very serious. Reactions range from feeling irritated to experiencing relapse or emotional breakdown. This is especially true for recovering addicts and alcoholics who on top of all the normal stresses of life have the added stress generated by recovery!

Stress is a natural by-product of recovery. Because the body is working hard to repair damage created during active addiction, you may experience aches and pains, mood swings, sleep disturbances, poor concentration, confusion, and irritability. These symptoms often continue for several months after one's last drink or drug use. As necessary as they are, these changes increase daily stress levels and play a huge role in determining the type of response choices we select. Increased sensitivity to stress may lead us to over- or underreact, and being preoccupied with recovery driven symptoms keeps us from recognizing signs of approaching stress overload until it's too late.

Negative self-talk further complicates this process by increasing stress levels that are already dangerously high. Individuals in early sobriety frequently interpret symptoms of early recovery negatively. Instead of acknowledging that things generally get worse before they get better, the newly sober tend to think: "Why am I going through all this, things have just gotten worse since I stopped drinking/using!" The combined effect of increasing symptoms and negative self-talk generates exhaustion and despair. Unless active steps are taken to interrupt this process, the individual will *inevitably* experience episodes of misdirected anger and relapse.

Before you lose hope, there *are* ways to redirect stress that will help you successfully move through the process of recovery. The first step involves developing a working knowledge of stress. Once you understand what stress is, that different types of stress exist, and that stress responses differ from person to person, you can build a personalized arsenal to combat it. Let's begin by defining the term *stress*. Stress is basically how the mind and body react when we feel threatened or afraid.

Seconds after we define something as potentially harmful the body goes into action preparing us to fight or run. Successful resolution of stress occurs when the actions taken by our bodies eliminate the source of stress or get us away from it (i.e., a water buffalo experiences terror when chased by a pack of hyenas. It instantly runs for its life. If successful, the water buffalo outruns its predator, recovers from this trauma, and goes back to grazing with no long-term ill effects). If, however, factors generating stress reactions cannot be resolved, or continue for long periods of time, the body eventually reaches a state of exhaustion resulting in serious illness or death.

With this definition in mind, does it necessarily mean *all stress* is bad and should be avoided? Look back at the example of the water buffalo for your answer. If that water buffalo had not been *stressed* to take flight when stalked by a pack of hyenas, it would be dead! A rather dramatic example, but I think you get the point. In "ordinary time" stress, depending on the circumstances, has the potential to create both positive and negative consequences. Determining whether stress is healthy or excessive requires us to revisit the exercise on triggers and cues (worksheet 2). The same triggers that set anger in motion (people, places, things, thoughts, feelings) also play a significant role in creating stress reactions. When triggers are *perceived* to be dangerous or threatening (whether they really are or not) your stress level skyrockets. These same factors, if perceived to be nonthreatening, leave stress levels virtually unaffected.

Successful stress management hinges on identifying *how* and *why* triggers developed (how things you perceive as stressful came to earn that definition) and recognizing *cues* activated by these triggers (what physical, emotional, cognitive, and behavioral reactions occur when you are exposed to identified triggers). Once this is accomplished you can evaluate the accuracy of existing beliefs: Are my reactions appropriate given the current circumstances? Am I over- or underreacting, and if so, what action is needed to redirect my behavior more productively? This is especially important during the early stages of recovery. Since newly sober individuals have difficulty accurately evaluating sources of stress, misinterpretation is a major risk factor for relapse and misdirected anger. It is often helpful to rely on family members, peers and professional therapists to assist you in this process until your perceptions become more accurate and predictable.

With this in mind, let's spend some time comparing the characteristics of healthy stress and distress (see table 2). Looking closely we discover the primary difference in healthy stress and distress is that one creates the potential for a balanced, sober life while the other almost always results in relapse. Simply stated this means healthy stress creates enough tension to keep us moving toward identified goals but not so much that we feel frustrated or overwhelmed. Distress, on the other hand, creates the same kind of reaction you get when driving on ice without snow chains or studded tires. If your car spins out of control you can't get enough traction to immediately correct the situation. The more frantically you try, the worse the situation gets. The only way to regain control is to patiently steer into the skid and avoid braking. Managing distress is very similar. Learning to identify warning signs prepares us to activate coping skills, reducing the risk of stress overload.

A number of warning signs appear as we move from healthy stress toward distress. To interrupt this process, we must first recognize symptoms that *most people* have when experiencing increasing distress. Second, we must learn to identify the role these factors play in our *personalized* reactions to stress (remember the triggers and cues worksheet in chapter 4). Finally, it is vital to understand the difference between short-term, chronic, and combined stress reactions and the impact each has on our ability to tolerate and successfully resolve stressful experiences. Only then can we successfully activate coping skills to defuse the anger–relapse cycle. Let's begin by identifying symptoms most people experience as they encounter stressful events. These fall into four main categories: physical complaints, changes in emotional states, changes in thinking, and changes in behavior. A closer examination of each category prepares us to identify *personalized* stress reactions (how these factors present themselves as *each individual* experiences stressful situations).

PHYSICAL COMPLAINTS

This includes changes in body functions that occur automatically when we experience stressful events. Headaches, backaches, muscle tension, increased blood pressure and heart rate, sweating, flushing, getting pale,

Table 2
Healthy Stress versus Distress

Healthy Stess	Distress
Promotes creative thinking	Creates a state of mental confusion
Creates pathways for personal growth	Sets up roadblocks to personal growth
Promotes productive risk taking (Willing to challenge unproductive patterns of response)	Interferes with productive risk taking (Resists challenging unproductive patterns of response)
Motivates and stimulates	Overwhelms and immobilizes
Improves self-esteem	Erodes self-esteem
Increases positive feelings and thoughts	Increases negative feelings and thoughts
Energizes and revitalizes	Leads to a state of exhaustion and despair
Creates opportunities	Derails opportunities
Creates a sense of inner peace	Creates turmoil and inner conflict
Helps create a balanced life-style	Creates a distorted sense of balance that leads to frustration and despair
Enhances the potential for assertive communication	Increases the potential for episodes of imploded or exploded anger
Supports sobriety by interrupting the anger–relapse cycle	Generates episodes of relapse and fuels the anger–relapse cycle

Note: Adapted from *Anger and addiction: Breaking the relapse cycle, a teaching guide for professionals*, by J. Clancy, 1996. Madison, CT: Psychosocial Press.

aches and pains in areas of our bodies that have been injured in the past, stomach aches, changes in breathing (faster/slower), and a host of other symptoms too numerous to mention.

We seldom notice these changes because they happen instinctively. Our awareness of these shifts generally occurs *after* the source of our distress is resolved and our bodies are attempting to return to their pre-stress state.

CHANGES IN EMOTIONAL STATE

This relates to shifts in mood created by real or perceived sources of distress (remember, if you *think* something is stressful, it *becomes* stressful). Feeling depressed, finding yourself overwhelmed by daily life events, and feeling more irritable than normal are all warning signs that the risk for stress overload is increasing. Rapid mood swings (you are feeling good and suddenly find yourself feeling angry, confused, hopeless, or scared for no reason) are also "red flags" of approaching stress overload. Learning to recognize "stress triggers" generating these mood swings is a vital step in breaking the anger–relapse cycle.

CHANGES IN THINKING

This takes us back to the issue of self-talk. "Listen" to the content of self-talk messages and monitor shifts that include excuses for why you *should* be angry, withdrawn, stressed out, take a drink, use drugs. When thinking takes a turn for the worse thoughts focus on how bad/wrong/ unjust our situation is. This causes us to lose sight of opportunities for resolution. It also leads to "worst outcome" thinking (this is the most terrible, horrible, awful thing that could ever happen, I'm doomed) which mentally increases our sense of approaching disaster.

Another clue that thoughts are moving us toward stress overload is when we blame everyone and everything for our problems without stopping to think about how these problems might be resolved (after all, if I run out of gas because my teenager doesn't fill the gas tank the *immediate problem* is how to get gas so I can keep moving, *not* whose fault it was that I ran out of gas. That comes later and *after* the use of timeout to redirect all those nasty thoughts of murder and mayhem! Right?). Again, these shifts in thinking are subtle and often catch us off-guard. Monitoring self-talk, and how it affects body reactions, mood, and behavior, provides another tool for interrupting the anger–relapse cycle.

CHANGES IN BEHAVIOR

This refers to how we act out (or in) our feelings and thoughts. Becoming uneasy (pacing, tapping fingers, opening and closing fists, gesturing, cursing, invading someone else's space, jumping up and down) are all signs of increasing stress. When we fail to recognize this tension buildup, the likely outcome is misdirected anger and relapse. Physical or emotional withdrawal (avoiding contact with family members and friends, not leaving the house, sleeping for 10 to 18 hours at a stretch, refusing to answer the phone or door, not keeping up with personal hygiene, procrastination, stuffing feelings, etc.) are also signs that stress levels are approaching the critical zone. These shifts in behavior are rarely noticed until we become so upset or withdrawn that others bring it to our attention. Learning to "read" behavior cues, along with emotional and cognitive cues, buys us time to mobilize coping skills to decrease or redirect tension. This can greatly reduce the risk of stress overload, misdirected anger, and relapse.

The physical, emotional, cognitive, and behavioral cues (symptoms) described above make up an "early warning system" that urges us to activate stress reduction strategies. These symptoms, and the order in which they appear, become particularly important as we attempt to understand *individual* reactions to stress. Four factors play a central role in activating stress cues and the responses we select to reduce or eliminate distress: our beliefs about the source of distress, personal tolerance levels for stress, the presence or absence of coping skills to resolve stressful events, and the nature of the situation creating distress (short-term, chronic, or a combination of the two). A closer look at these factors will explain how individual reactions to stress evolve.

OUR BELIEFS ABOUT THE SOURCE OF DISTRESS

Our *thoughts* about what is causing our distress greatly influence response choices. If we *believe* action can be taken to resolve a stressful situation, we will monitor our stress cues and take action to counteract the source of our distress. If, however, we feel powerless to change the situation, our sense of hopelessness leads to inaction and stress levels continue to rise. Let's look at an example to demonstrate the power of mind over matter.

THE CASE OF A BATTERED WIFE

Susan (not her real name) came to me very reluctantly on the advice of her employer. She was in a long-term marriage (20-plus years) to a man who had abused her throughout the course of the relationship. Her belief that the situation was her own fault, and could never change, trapped her in a situation that was fast becoming life-threatening. The level of abuse Susan's husband resorted to became more violent as the relationship continued. Initially, the abuse was verbal and emotional ("You'll never amount to anything, you always screw things up, you're such a pitiful example of a woman I only keep you because nobody else would put up with you . . ."). Over time, the abuse escalated to physical violence. First there were slaps and shoves, later, black eyes and bruises. The past 2 years had resulted in a broken arm and a broken collar bone. As the physical violence increased, the verbal and emotional abuse also continued. Susan's husband constantly threatened her. He told her nobody else would want her, that if she left she would die and that if she didn't die he would kill her. The event that finally brought her in for treatment was when her husband used an iron to "brand" her in multiple places on her body so she would know she was "his" property. Susan's employer was so concerned by the clearly visible and terribly painful results that she threatened to call the police unless Susan sought help.

Because Susan's beliefs about the source of her distress ("My husband only does these things to help me do better") were so firmly established, the mere mention of a women's shelter awoke extreme terror. The process of challenging and replacing the irrational belief that she somehow caused and deserved this abuse was a long, painful process for Susan. During early sessions she sat with her coat on, hat in hand, ready to flee at the first sign of danger (that I might somehow make her leave her husband). As time passed, she began to relax and talk more freely. Susan was raised in an abusive family and married young to escape being physically and sexually abused by her father. She had literally jumped out of the frying pan into the fire! Helping her identify this connection was critical since Susan could not leave an abusive relationship again without some hope that things could be different ("If I leave my husband the next situation might be even worse" needed to change to "Not all relationships are abusive, I deserve more than this").

Over the next 6 months, Susan attended both individual and group therapy sessions during work hours so her husband would not know she was seeking help. She gradually began making plans to leave her marriage. She was assisted in locating a women's shelter in a city nearby and met with staff to discuss options for safety and steps that could be taken to prevent her husband from attacking her (she had to keep her current job and he knew where she worked). The women's center helped Susan secure a restraining order and took active steps to safeguard her during the early stages of her separation. Her boss also gave her 2 weeks off so she could get through the initial crisis without being distracted by work.

Susan set a date to leave her marriage, and when the day arrived, she went with a constable and two staff members from the women's shelter to remove personal effects from her home. She left a note for her husband informing him that she had filed for divorce and that her lawyer would be in touch. Susan required a lot of support during the early months of her separation. Her husband made threatening phone calls to her place of business and showed up on several occasions demanding that she come with him. Since a restraining order was on file, the police were called and he was ordered to leave or face legal consequences. This created tremendous guilt and anxiety for Susan since her old thoughts were that *she* was to blame for the abuse so she should not punish her husband. It took great courage and the love and support of her employer and friends, along with professional counseling, to prepare Susan for this dramatic shift in how she lived her life.

As you can see in the above example, Susan's beliefs about the source of her stress ("I am abused because I deserve it") caused great emotional and physical pain. As time passed, and the abuse continued, Susan's belief was reinforced ("I really *must* be bad or this would not be happening to me"). It took a crisis (being burned multiple times with an iron and having her boss threaten to call the police) to get Susan to seek outside help. Even then it took another 6 months before she was able to leave this abusive relationship. Our *beliefs* about things that create stress in our lives *can and will hurt us* unless we figure out their *true* meaning. This often requires feedback from others. The moral: If you *question* whether your beliefs are valid it is a sign that they may not be—check it out with a friend, family member, or professional counselor before it is too late!

OUR PERSONAL TOLERANCE LEVEL FOR STRESS

This refers to how we, as individuals, tolerate events that most people would define as stressful. Personality type (high strung and easily upset or low key and seldom rattled) plays a big role in whether stress is *perceived* as manageable or ridiculous. A high-strung person (like Dr. Smith in the *Lost in Space* television series) often overreacts unnecessarily. People in this category unconsciously create 90 percent of their own stress by expecting the worst possible outcome (once again we see the strong connection between thoughts and behavior)! A person who is fairly level and takes things as they come is much better prepared to evaluate stress-inducing events and select reasonable responses.

Personal tolerance levels are influenced by our personality type; however, other factors also contribute to our overall tolerance for stress. Our general state of health, whether we have had a good night's sleep, are well fed, have adequate sources of emotional support, and coping skills with which to combat the stressor, all play a role in our ability to effectively manage stress. It makes sense that a person in good health, who is rested, fed, supported, and well versed in strategies for stress management, will fair better in stressful situations than will an individual who is ill, tired, hungry, isolated, and lacking in basic stress management skills (this topic will be addressed in chapter 11). Let's look at an example of the role personal stress tolerance levels play in responses to stress.

Just How Bad Is It—REALLY?

John and Elsa (not their real names) came in requesting help to resolve a financial crisis. John had worked steadily in a high-paying job for years and Elsa's income went for incidentals and luxury items. When John experienced a heart attack, he was unable to return to work for an indefinite period of time. Elsa suddenly became the family's bread winner. This drop in income made it impossible for the couple to continue their former life-style and they soon reached a point of financial distress (savings were used up and they had no way to immediately increase their monthly income). Although the stressful event (financial crisis) was identical for both individuals, their reactions were quite different based on personal stress tolerance levels.

Prior to his heart attack, John never missed a day of work in his life. He was high strung, fast paced, and had an attitude that, "if you want something done, do it yourself." He had few friends and used work as a means of defining himself as a "successful man." After several months of not working John became very depressed. He felt helpless to change the situation since he could not return to work without risking further physical consequences (another heart attack). John found this experience highly stressful because it challenged his belief about his role as a man and provider for his family. Since he had few friends, he bottled up his feelings, which only increased his sense of hopelessness and despair. John became short-tempered and used alcohol in an attempt to cope with the emotional strain produced by his physical condition and the resulting financial crisis.

Elsa's approach was much different. She was easy going and had an attitude of, "Well, let's see what needs to be done and do it." She seldom got flustered and relied on family members and friends for emotional support and guidance. After John's heart attack, Elsa readily took over the task of earning funds to meet family expenses. She reasoned, "Thank God John is still alive. That's all that really matters. We can get through the financial crisis, it just means we'll have to adjust our lifestyle so my income can support us." Elsa's personality type, combined with her good health and active use of available support networks, kept her stress at a manageable level while John struggled with daily panic attacks, alcohol abuse, and outbursts of anger.

As demonstrated in the above example, personal tolerance levels for stress can lead to very different results. If you happen to be a high-strung individual like John, don't despair! Chapter 11 provides ideas for counteracting this factor so stressful events can be approached and resolved more productively.

The Presence or Absence of Coping Skills Needed to Resolve Sources of Stress

Simply stated, this means do we know how and what to do when stressful events occur. If we have a number of tools for coping with stress (time-out, problem solving, seeking the support of a family member or friend, exercise, redirection of our thoughts and activities), our potential to successfully approach and resolve stressful events is high. Successful outcomes, in turn, boost self-esteem and reinforce sobriety. If, however, coping skills are lacking or inadequate, we are at great risk of resorting to patterns of behavior that, although self-destructive, are uncomfortably familiar (overeating, drinking, using drugs, acting out, withdrawing). This, in turn, damages self-esteem and interferes with efforts to achieve and sustain long-term, quality sobriety. Let's look at an example of how coping skills affect stress levels *and* sobriety.

MY WAY OR THE HIGHWAY

James (not his real name) is a 50-year-old man who has *always* done things *his way*. He lives where he wants, drinks whatever and whenever he wants, sees whom he wants, and only does what he wants. This way of life worked fairly well for James *until* he received a third DWI charge. The judge chastised him soundly for his reckless, irresponsible behavior and offered him one last chance to redeem himself. He ordered James to attend an alcohol treatment program and told him if he failed to complete the program, his probation would be revoked and he would be sent to prison.

James, as you can imagine, was *not* happy with this ultimatum. After all, who was this @@##** judge to tell *him* what he could and couldn't do! He enrolled in treatment with a hostile, defensive, threatening attitude and stated, "I'm here cause I have to be but I don't plan to do @#*@!" James was informed of clinic policies, including daily urine screens. He was instructed to sign a release of information so reports could be made to his probation officer. Although angry, James agreed since the alternative was a prison cell. James attended group sessions faithfully and had negative urine screens throughout the first month of his admission. He also remained hostile and distant, stating, "I can play this game, but as soon as it's over party time here I come!" James refused to even consider that another way of thinking and behaving might exist and continued to attend without participating.

After one month of treatment, his case was reviewed by the clinical team. The team agreed that although James attended regularly and had negative urine screens, he was not benefiting from treatment, and in fact, was harmful to other patients' recovery since he frequently made negative comments in group. James was seen by the team and informed that if his attitude and participation did not change, he would be irregularly discharged from the program and a report sent to his probation officer. He was reminded that treatment would only work if *he* wanted it to. He was encouraged to think about it over the weekend and advise the team of his decision the following Monday.

When James attended group on Monday, he immediately began to blame the leader for threatening to throw him out of the program. To the leader's surprise group members began to confront James with his negative, hostile behavior. Several members shared how they too had entered treatment against their wishes but had come to understand how and why they continued to use alcohol even when it created negative consequences. This powerful session was a turning point in James' treatment. He broke down in tears as stories of past childhood physical and sexual abuse poured out. By the end of the session James admitted that he had "gotten tough" to survive in a world that had tortured and abused him.

Although far from being a "changed man" James agreed to stop making negative comments and at least keep an open mind. Over the course of the next year James made good progress in confronting self-destructive patterns of thinking and behaving. He developed coping skills that helped him maintain sobriety and successfully cope with stressful events. Not all cases have such a positive outcome. However, James' case *clearly* demonstrates how the presence or absence of coping skills can make or break an individual's ability to get through stressful events without returning to former patterns of self-defeating behavior.

THE NATURE OF THE SITUATION CREATING DISTRESS

This final factor refers to whether an individual is experiencing situations that create short-term, chronic, or combined stress reactions (see Table 3 and model 7). An overview of these stress reactions, and their effect on *stress cues* and *personalized response choices* will conclude chapter 10.

Short-Term Stressors

This category refers to stressful events that create *minor* disturbances in daily life. Examples include:

- A run in your pantyhose
- You just can't get your tie even (and don't have a clip-on)
- You put your power saw in a "safe place" and now you can't find it.
- Your curling iron shorts out when your hair is only half curled.

Table 3
Comparison of Stress Reactions

Short-Term Stress	Chronic Stress	Combined Stress
A stressful event that is mild or moderate in nature occurs	A stressful event that is moderate to severe in nature occurs	The individual is in a delayed state of recovery due to the chronic stress in his or her life when short-term stress occurs
Coping skills are mobilized and stressors resolved without taxing energy reserves. Additional energy remains available for other activities	Coping skills are mobilized; however, the stressor is chronic in nature and cannot be easily resolved. Tension continues to build as the individual struggles to regain control	The individual immediately experiences stress overload and is unable to mobilize coping skills needed to resolve the stressor
The individual experiences a brief recovery period, during which body functions, emotional state, thoughts, and behavior return to normal	Reserve energies are called into use and exhausted. This forces the individual to extend themselves beyond safe limits	After repeated attempts to resolve the stressor, a marginal resolution is achieved. The individual, energy reserves depleted, remains at risk for future trauma due to the absence of available coping skills and/or the energy to mobilize them
No long-term effects are experienced, and the individual continues with their normal activities	Stress overload occurs. There is no more energy to effectively cope. Once the stressor is finally resolved, a delayed recovery period begins. The individual is highly susceptible to physical illness, emotional distress, misdirected anger, and relapse	Attempts to return to the pre-stress level of functioning are challenged by daily life stressors creating a sense of hopelessness and despair. Risk of relapse and misdirected anger are extreme

- You lock your keys in the car.
- You forget to "Spring forward" when daylight saving time begins and are late to work.
- You have a sick child and have to miss work.
- Your cable TV goes out.
- You have a minor illness like a cold or sinus infection.

Model 7: Stress Reactions

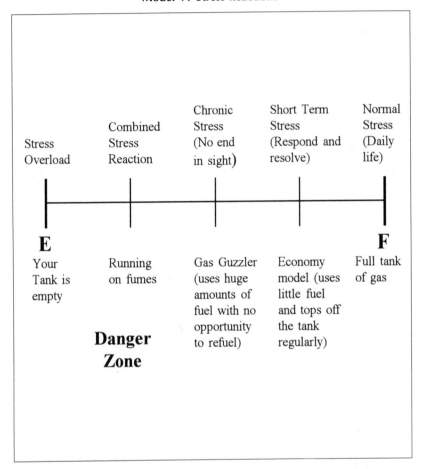

- Your child tells you they need school supplies—at 10:30 P.M. the night before they are due!
- You have a job interview or project deadline.

Yes, these situations can be anxiety provoking and annoying; however, they do not create major shifts in the course of our destiny! Short-term stress is generally mild to moderate in nature and stimulates us to take action to resolve it. We experience *minor* changes in physical cues (heart rate goes up, breathing increases, etc.), in mood (feeling irritated about being inconvenienced), thoughts (thinking what a pain life can be at times), and behavior (we raise our voices/get quiet, move a little quicker/ slower, appear more restless) and quickly return to our prestress state after resolving the issue at hand.

Analogies Include

1. Carrying a half full cup of coffee across the room and tripping on the area rug. I may stumble but avoid falling *and* manage not to spill the coffee.
2. Hitting a small pothole in the road. I feel the bump, make adjustments to straighten out my car, and go about my business.

CHRONIC STRESSORS

This category includes stressful experiences that create *major* disturbances in our lives. Examples include:

- Long-term unemployment (seeking but cannot find a job).
- Financial pressures—large debts with no way to repay them.
- Chronic physical or mental illness in self or family members.
- *Active addiction.*
- An abusive relationship that you just can't find the courage to leave.
- Being a caregiver for someone who is ill or disabled.
- Role strain (trying to wear too many hats at once and not knowing how to take some of them off).
- Social isolation.
- Illiteracy (being unable to read and too ashamed to ask for help so you carefully hide "the secret" no matter what the emotional cost).
- Multiple losses occurring close together (within a one-year period you get divorced, your parents die, you lose your job).

Chronic stressors change the course of our destiny, often in dramatic and irreversible ways! These stressors use up large amounts of physical and emotional energy, often without achieving the desired result. Although many of these stressors can be resolved across time, the individual facing them becomes so overwhelmed and confused he or she stops trying. The result: Their stress levels continue to rise. Chronic stress creates *strong to severe* shifts in our physical cues (ulcers, migraine headaches, high blood pressure, recurring infections); mood (depression, hopelessness, anger, terror); thoughts (this is more than I can bear, if I kill myself it will all be over; I will never be able to dig my way out of this, I feel like I'm suffocating); and behavior (drink, use drugs, run away, act out, or die). Even if we eventually resolve the stressor, we are so exhausted that little emotional energy remains available to cope with other stressors that might arise.

Analogies Include

1. Carrying a full cup of coffee across the room and tripping on the area rug. I spill coffee all over the place and burn my hand. The mess can be cleaned up and my hand will heal, but I end up with a permanent scar!
2. Hitting a big pothole in the road. I lose control of my car and have to work hard to avoid an accident. I also throw the car out of alignment so I have to put it in the shop for repairs to avoid further damage.

COMBINED STRESSORS

This category refers to situations where we experience chronic stress and are exhausted and overwhelmed. A short-term stressor is added, sending us into stress overload. We are so busy trying to resolve the chronic stressor we don't even see the short-term stressor coming. We get sideswiped before knowing what happened. This experience further damages self-esteem and increases the risk of misdirected anger and relapse. Examples include:

- Trying to cope with financial pressures and having your child ask for a trip to Astroworld.
- Long-term unemployment and the person standing next to you in the line at the unemployment office says, "I just lost my job but only people who don't want to work stay unemployed. I hope to be working again by next week."
- Being the single head of household with four children and being told "Sorry, you miss the foodstamp eligibility cut-off by three dollars."

- Having a chronic psychiatric illness and having someone question what you do with your "free time" since you don't work.
- Feeling pressurized by a life-style with too many commitments and having someone ask you to volunteer for anything—especially if it involves your children!
- Struggling with active addiction and having an "associate" say, "Come on man, what's one more drink in the larger scheme of things."
- Living in an abusive relationship and having your child get sick (in the past this has triggered episodes of abuse because, "If you were a better parent that kid would not be sick")!
- You are socially isolated due to illness or disability and your only connection with the world is through your television—your cable TV goes out.
- You are illiterate and constantly on guard lest someone find out. You attend a parents' night at your child's school and are asked to read a list of awards.

Combined stress reactions can be devastating because we are already so overwhelmed and preoccupied that we fail to see them coming. Shifts in physical, emotional, cognitive, and behavioral cues occur swiftly and are often extreme, creating a sense of panic. The potential for overreaction is *huge* and in turn creates even more stress. Since people rarely know about our *chronic* stressors unless they are a close friend or relative, these overreactions to what appear to be small issues, lead others to judge us harshly. This seriously damages self-esteem and provides excuses for resorting to alcohol, drugs, and other forms of self-destructive behavior to "ease the pain "

Analogies Include

1. Walking across the room with an overflowing cup of coffee that is slopping over the edges with every step I take. I am so busy trying to prevent spilling any more coffee that I trip over the area rug, lose my balance, fall, and spill scalding coffee all over myself. I end up with several permanent scars.
2. Driving down a road, I see a *huge* pothole at the last possible minute before hitting it. I swerve to miss it and hit an even bigger pothole

breaking an axle. My car is disabled to the point I need a tow and it will cost several hundred dollars to repair.

When comparing short-term, chronic, and combined sources of stress, we could easily say that short-term stresses are "no big deal" so why worry about them. The tendency to diminish small sources of stress creates the same result as ignoring stress cues, imploding anger, and failing to heed "tiny" cravings—we continue down the path toward destruction until the situation is so bad we *have to* acknowledge it. Think of short-term stresses as pennies are to dollars. If I look at the value of one little penny in 1996 it doesn't even seem worth picking up. If, however, I see the "bigger picture," I realize that if I save pennies long enough I will eventually have a dollar. Stress has the same potential to build up over time, and without intervention inevitably leads to episodes of misdirected anger, and relapse. In chapter 11 we will identify ways to manage situations involving short-term, chronic, and combined stress.

11

Life's Too Short

In the previous chapter we defined stress, explored personal reactions to stress, and identified different types of stress that affect us as we move through life experiences. At this point the million dollar question is, "Now that we know all we ever (never) wanted to know about stress, *how do we manage it without relapsing or going crazy?*" Three primary tasks are necessary to accomplish this goal. We must:

1. Identify our personal responses to stress (how and why we respond as we do).
2. Create *and be willing to activate* our personal arsenal of stress reduction tools.
3. Regularly review the effectiveness of these tools, making changes as needed, to strengthen our existing plan.

Because individual reactions to stress are very different, it is important to identify your personal response style *before* designing a stress management plan. Just as you would select weapons for war based on your enemy's firepower, the design and content of your stress management plan should be determined by factors that influence your personal response choices. To begin this process, let's review the concept of stress tolerance levels introduced in chapter 10. Remember that stress tolerance levels are greatly affected by personality type. If you are high strung and impatient, it is unlikely that, after learning stress reduction tools, you will suddenly become a low-key, easygoing person. Likewise, if you are a person who has been fairly even-tempered all your life, you are unlikely to become a live wire after entering recovery. Although we cannot change "core" personality characteristics (once a turtle always a turtle, once a hare always a hare), we *can* learn to recognize and redirect negative responses stemming from personality traits. The following examples help illustrate this process.

EXAMPLE ONE: "I'LL BE THERE WHEN I GET THERE"

If you are an individual who is always late, it may affect your ability to maintain employment, relationships, and other activities that demand promptness and reliability. Part of learning to effectively manage stress created by chronic tardiness is to first identify *why* you are chronically late. Self-statements like, "Oh, well, this is just how I am and people will have to get used to it," are frequently involved. These unconscious self-statements imply that you have no control over tardiness since, "It's just the way you are." One way to fight these self-defeating messages is to accept *personal responsibility* for arriving places on time *in spite of your personality type*! Taking responsibility for "making it happen" allows you to challenge existing beliefs and replace them with productive alternatives: "Well, this is how I am but it sure gets in the way. How can I work with this personality trait and get where I'm going on time?" Ideas include laying out clothes and items needed for the next day *before* going to bed, setting the alarm clock 30 minutes earlier to make up for the tendency to put things off, and developing self-rewards for being on time (like being able to sleep in on your day off, not having to set an alarm clock or wear a watch on weekends).

EXAMPLE TWO: "I SHOULD HAVE BEEN THERE YESTERDAY"

The same process works in reverse for high-strung individuals. If you are driven to arrive early and have anxiety attacks at the mere thought of arriving "right on time" or late, the first step in changing this tendency to overreact is identifying *why* you feel so pressured to arrive early. Again, this involves accepting *personal responsibility* for monitoring and challenging self-talk messages. What do you tell yourself about arriving late? Unconscious messages from our past like, "Only rude, lazy, irresponsible people arrive late; if you're late terrible things will happen," can generate extreme levels of unnecessary stress. This, in turn, is a setup for relapse: "Boy was that stressful, I think I'll have a drink, smoke a joint, to calm down." You might practice arriving "on time" or slightly late to see what happens. Rarely will the world end if you are late (unless, of course, you are attending the ballet and don't want to miss the first act)! More often than not, nobody will even notice if you are 5 or 10 minutes late. The more you practice this skill, the more control you will have over those racehorse tendencies *and* your stress level!

Whether we are healthy, well rested, and adequately nourished also affects our tolerance for stress. Human beings on the whole tend to be more irritable and reactive when we are ill, tired, or hungry. These physical sources of stress cloud our ability to properly consider and respond to the demands of daily living. This is especially true for the newly sober whose bodies are damaged from the abuse and neglect that occurred during active addiction. Therefore, one of the first steps in stress management for recovering addicts and alcoholics is developing healthy lifestyle practices.

Finally, the presence or absence of emotional support, *and our willingness to use this resource in times of crisis*, plays an important role in stress tolerance levels. Although we would like to believe we can manage our lives without outside support, there comes a time in *everyone's* life where help is needed. *Nobody* can do it alone *all the time* (no matter how macho, strong, self-reliant, invincible you are)! I would say that even Atlas (the Greek God who carried the world on his shoulders) set the world down, or leaned against a wall, when he thought nobody was looking! Having an available source of support becomes especially important during early stages of recovery. Stress can quickly lead to relapse unless a strong support network is available 24 hours a day. The value of 12-step groups and sponsors during this critical time in recovery cannot be overemphasized!

Once factors influencing individual stress tolerance levels are determined, we can move to the next stage of developing a personalized stress management plan: identifying and evaluating existing and potential strategies with which to combat stress. From the time we are infants we *unconsciously* develop coping skills as stressful events are encountered. Our repertoire of coping skills develops through exposure to role models during childhood (watching how they manage their stress), and by trial and error (whether our responses worked/did not work in the past). Across time, these patterns of response become so natural we seldom think about them unless someone questions our motives for responding as we do. Indeed, most of us go through life repeatedly applying the same coping skills, never stopping to consider whether these skills worked in the past, whether they are currently working, or whether another approach might be more productive/less costly.

When evaluating current and possible stress management strategies it is *vital* to weigh potential benefits and costs of *each* identified coping skill. I cannot overstate the ongoing nature of this process! Coping skills should be evaluated on a regular basis (or whenever life circumstances change) to assure their continued success. The following analogy highlights the importance of ongoing evaluation. If my car is 2 years old, has 26,000 miles, and needs a tune-up, I would be better off performing the routine maintenance than trading it in for a newer car. When that same car reaches 10 years of age, has 200,000 miles, and needs $1000 in repairs, I would be better off trading it in. The only way I will know whether the car has reached the point of diminishing returns (costing more than it gives back) is to evaluate its cost to performance ratio on an *annual* basis!

In addition to evaluating the current effectiveness of coping skills, we must also monitor how often and how long we continue to apply specific coping skills. While intensive involvement in treatment is positive during early stages of recovery, treatment should gradually decrease to a maintenance level with "booster visits" during periods of extreme stress or crisis. Failure to consider continued application of a coping skill beyond its initial period of usefulness can lead to "addiction swapping." Have you ever been to an AA meeting? They don't drink alcohol but smoke is so thick you can cut it and the coffee pot is ever flowing! In the initial stages of sobriety I encourage a newly sober person *not* to stop smoking cigarettes or drinking coffee so they can focus on maintaining abstinence from alcohol. However, after they achieve one year of sobriety I encourage them to address their nicotine and caffeine addictions! Failing to question *why* we continue to follow certain patterns of behavior is habit forming (remember the story of the ham). The result: Coping skills get out of date, setting us up for episodes of misdirected anger and relapse. This is really scary if we think about medical advances—what if doctors never had to participate in continuing education courses? Would *you* feel safe letting a doctor trained in 1915 who *never received training after graduation* do open heart surgery on *your* heart!! Well, since open heart surgery was unheard of at that time, neither would I! Get the point?

To complicate matters further, many coping skills have the potential to generate both positive and negative outcomes, depending on where they are put to use, and the intensity and length of their application (how, where, and under what circumstances they are activated). Individuals who "overuse" certain coping skills to the point of diminishing returns often continue to defend their use even after negative consequences occur. Let's look at a few examples of how innocently this transition from what might be viewed as a positive coping skill can suddenly become negative.

- *Workaholics* "look" healthier than alcoholics and drug addicts and often justify their behavior by saying, "I can't believe you're complaining—I stopped drinking/using and I work this hard so *you* can have advantages in life." In reality, they switched one addiction (drinking) for another (excessive working) without considering *why* they must participate in *any* form of addictive behavior. A 40-hour work week is a healthy coping skill. When it becomes an 80-hour week, it is addictive in nature. Workaholics often "tune out" comments that their lack of involvement in family relationships is identical to when they were drinking. Unfortunately, by the time others finally get their attention, damage to family relationships, friendships, health, and mental health is often beyond repair.
- *Exercise and dieting* "appear" healthy, and if done cautiously produce a fit and healthy body. If, however, people exercise four, five, eight hours a day, starve themselves, or throw up after eating to maintain an ultrathin appearance, it can create life-threatening conditions.
- *Taking time out* to think about your options is a healthy, productive response. If, however, you begin using time-out as an excuse to avoid communicating with others, or stuff feelings, it becomes a destructive process that leads to isolation, imploded anger, and relapse!

As stated earlier, developing a personalized stress management plan that reduces stress and supports sobriety is an ongoing process. This process must be repeated each time we experience major life changes (enter a new phase of life, experience a loss, experience an expected or unexpected change in our life-style—raise, demotion, divorce, marriage, have a baby, have a child leave home). The following exercise will help you identify current stress management strategies, stimulate ideas for new coping skills you might not have considered, and provide opportunities to consider how what appears to be positive (or negative) might be used to your best advantage (see Worksheet 6, pp. 157–158).

After completing worksheet 6, look to see how many positive and negative coping skills you identified. Remember, even positives can become destructive if overused! Let's spend some time looking at potential misuse of positives and how to avoid this trap and then we'll focus our energies on identifying how to replace negative responses with more productive alternatives (refer to tables 4 and 5).

Worksheet 6 and tables 4 and 5 will provide you with a better understanding of why it is so important to identify current coping skills, regularly review their effectiveness, and make conscious efforts to challenge and replace self-destructive methods of managing stress with more productive alternatives. This is a difficult process which requires patience, a sense of humor, and commitment to change. Let's turn now to a final strategy for coping with stressful situations: *humor.*

Humor can provide valuable comic relief even in the most intense situations. Learning to laugh at ourselves and life situations, even when they are not very funny, can provide the strength we need to "get through" these experiences. When faced with stressful events we are initially so stunned and numb that feelings are blocked. Humor can provide an outlet for pent-up tension until we recover enough to begin the grieving process. An example might help you better understand this process.

ROSCO THE TURTLE

When my husband and I were newly married he was involved in a child custody dispute with his ex-wife. This was an expensive, highly stressful experience that often left us feeling tense, distant, and overwhelmed. At

Table 4
When Positives Become Negatives

Correct Use of Positive Coping Skills	Misuse of Positive Coping Skills
1. Listen to music for brief periods of time to relax and recover	1. Use music to escape from reality
2. Redirect your activity to disrupt negative self-talk	2. Redirect your activity to avoid dealing with the problem now or later
3. Take a short nap	3. Sleep to escape
4. Participate in an activity you enjoy to "recharge your batteries"	4. Participate in an activity you enjoy to avoid addressing the problem
5. Practice meditation, or deep breathing to relax and regroup	5. Practice meditation or deep breathing to avoid uncomfortable issues
6. Take a time-out to think about options	6. Take a time-out and avoid thinking about the problem
7. Openly express feelings/ask for support	7. Share only "safe feelings" to avoid offers of support from others
8. Take a shower or bath to relieve tension	8. Take a shower or bath to avoid issues you don't want to address
9. Do a good deed for someone else to boost your morale	9. Do a good deed to avoid addressing your own issues
10. Exercise, jog, or walk to relax and release tension	10. Excessive use of exercise as an escape
11. Visit or call a friend for support and advice	11. Visit or call a friend in worse shape than you to make you feel stronger
12. Give yourself permission to be silly for comic relief	12. Use silly behavior to mask underlying emotional pain
13. Write in a diary or journal to help identify "stuck points"	13. Write for the sake of writing with no goal in mind
14. Read a book or magazine in short intervals to relax	14. Read to escape

Table 5
Turning Negatives into Positives

Current Use of Negative Coping Skills	Redirecting Negative Coping Skills
1. Avoid social contact with others	1. Brief periods of "alone time" to think followed by contact with a friend
2. Overeat, eat junk food, skip meals	2. Occasional "rewards" of junk foods after eating a good meal
3. Use alcohol or drugs	3. Have a refreshing fruit drink
4. Spend money you don't have to spare	4. Go to the dollar movie or window shop with a friend
5. Blame others for your problems	5. Take a time-out and assess the problem, NOT who is to blame
6. Drive fast and recklessly	6. Run, walk, or exercise to work off tension
7. Sleep to escape	7. Take a short nap, then call a friend
8. Sit and feel sorry for yourself	8. Have a 5 minute "pity party" then spend 5 minutes adding up the positives in your life
9. Drink excessive amounts of coffee	9. Have a cup of decaf with a friend
10. Become irritable and use abusive language with others	10. Try saying silly words like "Oh horse KAKA" or "Oh retention wall"
11. Smoke tobacco	11. Chew on a carrot stick, have a candy cigarette, use your nicorette gum
12. Think about suicide	12. Take a time-out and realize nothing lasts forever. Neither will your wish to die
13. Anticipate the worst possible outcome	13. Anticipate the best possible outcome

one point my husband made an appointment to consult a custody specialist in Dallas, about 300 miles from our home. The ride started off very tense when suddenly he slammed on the brakes, jumped out of the truck, and ran back toward the direction we had come. I was totally surprised, not knowing what to think. Soon after, my new husband came running up with a box turtle. When I asked what he was doing he said, "It was going to get run over, I just had to save it."

Believe it or not that turtle saved our sanity! It was a great distraction from the intense stress of the moment and provided multiple opportunities for comic relief. Once Rosco realized we meant him no harm he began peeking out of his shell. By the end of the day he would extend his neck and let me gently stroke him without retreating. I held him up to the window and sang goofy songs to him about passing billboards for over 200 miles of that 600-mile round trip! Looking back it seems like really crazy behavior. What I had done, not knowing how or why, was apply humor to an extremely stressful situation during a time when we had no time to grieve. We kept Rosco as a pet for several months and finally released him back to the wild on our property in Palestine.

WHERE'S THE DIPSTICK?

In 1990 my family experienced the loss of my brother-in-law to cancer. As his death approached I made arrangements to fly to California to say good-bye and offer emotional support to my sister. As you can imagine, this was a very intense time and the last thought in my mind was humor. On the day that was to be his last, we said our good-byes and went to my sister's home. There was nothing we could do at the hospital and we could not bear to sit and watch Jerry die. My mother, sister, her two best friends, and I became more anxious as the evening wore on. The call from the hospital could come at any time and every minute seemed like a year. Around midnight the tension was so intense that we decided to change the oil in my sister's Toyota van. If you have never owned one of these vans, let me tell you, it's an act of courage to change the oil in one! The engine is located under the front seats and you practically have to dismantle the van to get to the dipstick and oil filter. Struggling with this task we all started laughing hysterically. Tears streamed down our faces as we realized how ridiculous we must look, five women in pajamas, huddled around the partially dismantled van looking for a dipstick. We realized our "crazy" behavior was keeping us sane. The last few hours before Jerry's death were very painful so the distraction of humor was a welcome relief. When the call finally came we had released enough tension to cope with the grief that followed in our laughter's footsteps.

Although humor could not blot out or undo this terrible loss, it helped get us through that long and painful night.

HELLO! I'M MR. POTTY

Anyone who has ever raised a child will agree that potty training is one of the most challenging (and hair raising) experiences of parenthood. My youngest son has been especially resistant to this process. He will sit briefly (30 seconds or less) on his potty and say, "Tee-tee Mr. Potty," then stands up, says no with great determination, and pees on the rug! He is also fond of throwing poor Mr. Potty down the stairs, in the bathtub, and anywhere else he thinks we might not be able to recover this "device of torture."

As an older parent this time around I decided that humor was definitely the way to go. I remember 15 years ago when I trained my oldest son it was a grim, serious event. This battle of wills and my *insistence* that he learn to use the potty when *I* decided he was ready, resulted in battles that I *always* lost! This time I'm being more creative. I pretend that "Mr. Potty's" seat is a mouth and while moving the seat and lid, carry on conversations like "Hi Vincent, it's Mr. Potty—do you want to sit on me?" "Vincent, Mr. Potty will be your best friend if you sit on me." "Poor Mr. Potty—I'm so cold and lonely, will you please sit on me?"

Although the challenge continues even as I write, it is *much* less stressful and at times funny. Humor, combined with listening to and directing my self-talk, has helped me realize that potty training is not the life and death situation I thought it was 15 years ago. Vincent will *surely* be potty trained before his senior prom, so why sweat it. Patience, keeping my sense of humor, and continuing to have "Mr. Potty" state the advantages of being potty trained will eventually get us out of the "diaper years." Life is filled with stressful events, and practicing what I teach, I take every opportunity to "lighten up" with humor in situations that permit it—and even in some that don't! Who knows, instead of horror stories about potty training Vincent and I will probably laugh someday about his "talking potty"—maybe when *he* is potty training my grandchildren and needs a laugh!

When I teach my anger management/relapse prevention classes, one session is devoted to fun and games. I talk about the use of humor to release tension and promote recovery, *then* I actually have my clients sing and play in group. One of the first times I did this the group didn't know *how* to respond, so it went along. There were 18 people in the room and we created a stimulating version of *Old McDonald Had a Farm*. There were so many verses, people started writing them down and helping one another. By session's end the room was filled with laughter. We later heard we disrupted *every group in the clinic*! We also heard from other clients *not* in our group that they wished they had been!

Although being "silly" often makes us feel self-conscious, it is a very important part of our emotional survival. All children play and laugh naturally—it's a shame they (we) "learn" to be "more appropriate," as they (we) grow up. These "learned" messages about humor and silliness being "kids play" gradually and unconsciously rob us of the playfulness so vital to emotional survival. These messages shut down a powerful resource for coping with stress and emotional pain. Only *you* can unlock the door to the lighter side of who you used to be. I wholeheartedly encourage you to challenge faulty self-talk messages about what it means when adults are silly and replace them with the statement, "My inner child wants to come out and play and he or she deserves to: na-na, na-na, boo-boo!!"

In closing this chapter I want to impart some final "words of wisdom" as they relate to stress and the anger–relapse cycle:

1. Heed your parents' advice: A healthy diet, adequate rest, exercise, and a support network do wonders to minimize the disabling impact of stress. It also reduces the temptation to take it out on others or use stress as a "convenient excuse" to relapse.
2. Maintain a positive attitude and remain open to new ideas and experiences. Stress can mean *crisis* or *opportunity*. Make stress work for rather than against you.
3. Avoid becoming too serious. Make funny faces, skip down the street, play a childhood game. Taking breaks from responsibility prepares us for stressful situations yet to come.
4. Resist the temptation to compare yourself with others. There is no right or wrong way to approach distress, only differences in how we view and resolve it.
5. Monitor your self-talk. When negative messages creep in make conscious efforts to reroute thoughts in a positive direction. Our thoughts are a powerful resource for managing stress once we learn to harness and direct them.

6. Remember you have the right to set your own pace. Asking for what you want or need and learning to say no are powerful allies in the war against stress.
7. Sidestep the urge to reject help during times of extreme stress. Pride becomes an excuse to play Atlas. Since no person can stand alone in all situations, this attitude wields a deadly blow to sobriety.
8. Finally, and most importantly, be your own best friend. Selfishly guard your peace of mind and take active steps to create an environment that promotes happiness. Until you accomplish this objective, quality sobriety is an unattainable dream.

WORKSHEET 6

ASSESSING OPTIONS FOR MANAGING STRESS

This worksheet is designed to help you identify current and potential strategies for managing stressful events. Review the positive and negative coping skills wheels below and on the following page. Circle strategies you currently use (or have used in the past) to manage your stress. After completing both wheels, count the number of positive versus negative coping skills you circled. If you identified more negatives than positives, don't despair! Practice the skills introduced in this chapter and make a conscious effort to identify and replace each negative coping skill with a positive. Before you know it you will be on the road to successful stress management.

WHEEL OF POSITIVE COPING SKILLS

Watch T.V.
Go to the movies

Read a book or
magazine

Listen to music

Write in a
journal or diary

Redirect your
activity

Give yourself
permission to
play and be silly
(alone or with
someone)

Take a short
nap

**POSITIVE
STRESS
MANAGEMENT
STRATEGIES**

Other (You
Identify)

Participate in
an activity you
find relaxing
and fun

Practice
meditation or
deep breathing

Visit or call a
friend

Take time-out
to think about
options

Exercise, walk,
or jog

Openly express
feelings/ask for
support

Do a good
deed for
someone else

Take a shower or bath

Adapted, with permission of the publisher, from *Stress management participant's manual*, by D. Muntz, 1983. St. Louis: St. Louis University Medical Center-Healthline.

Worksheet 6 (continued)

WHEEL OF NEGATIVE COPING SKILLS

Avoid social contact with others

Anticipate the worst possible outcome

Think about suicide

Overeat or eat junk food, skip meals

Smoke tobacco

Use alcohol/drugs

Become irritable or use abusive language with others

Spend money you don't have to spare

NEGATIVE STRESS MANAGEMENT STRATEGIES

Drink excessive amounts of coffee

Blame others for your problems

Sit and feel sorry for yourself

Drive fast and reckless

Other (You identify)

Sleep as an escape

A. How many positive strategies did you circle? _____

B. How many negative strategies did you circle? _____

C. If you circled more negatives than positives, what steps can you take to redirect your negative responses? _____

_____

_____

Adapted, with permission of the publisher, from *Stress management participant's manual*, by D. Muntz, 1983. St. Louis: St. Louis University Medical Center-Healthline.

12

Beware of Exploding Potatoes

Microwave ovens are a marvelous invention! I remember when a baked potato used to take an hour and a half to cook. Well, no more! Microwave ovens produce a fully cooked potato in 8 minutes or less. There is, however, a catch. You have to know *how* to cook a potato in the microwave or look out! I'll never forget the first time I tried it! I scrubbed the potato, placed it inside the microwave, and pushed high for 8 minutes. After about 5 minutes I heard a loud noise and went running to the kitchen. The potato was all over the inside of my microwave! Nobody warned me that when pressure builds up inside a microwave it can cause potatoes to explode *unless* you poke holes in them for steam to vent. Since that experience I have *never* forgotten to poke holes in my potato *before* pressing "cook"!

So how does this story relate to anger and relapse? If you think about the contents of this book, a constant theme has been learning to select response choices that help you stay sober and vent anger sensibly. When this is not accomplished the result is relapse. Stuffed anger, like steam inside a potato with no vent holes, continues to build. If not redirected, it eventually turns into resentment: bitterness about life experiences that we cannot undo and will not let go of.

Resentments arise when we *repeatedly* fail to identify and express feelings and needs to ourselves and others and refuse to allow others to share

159

feelings and needs with us. Resentments create tunnel vision focused on the past (kind of like riding a horse backward—you are so busy seeing where you've been that you forget to look where you are and where you are going)! The tension that results from repeatedly withholding the need to share feelings and needs with others ultimately activates the anger–relapse cycle. Managing resentments means remembering and letting go of (not forgetting) past experiences that reach into the here-and-now and prevent us from moving on with life. This involves recognizing the buildup process (refer back to your "Triggers and Cues" worksheet) and applying coping skills to "vent off" tension before we end up like the exploded potato!

We often think we are "doing ourselves and others a favor" by stuffing anger. A common theme in my anger management/relapse prevention training group is, "Jo, if we tell people how we feel it will hurt them *or* they will use it against us. It's better to just keep quiet." The flaw with this belief is that stuffed anger does not simply "go away." If you keep anger bottled up inside pressure continues to build leading to depression, negative self-talk, and a sense of hopelessness about life (why bother, things will never change). If you are an explosive person, pent-up anger finally erupts, usually when and where you least expect it! Instead of reducing the risk of hurting others you relapse which hurts them even more. An example might help you understand how something that seems so harmless can create such negative results.

Springtime is a time of bright flowers, cool, crisp mornings, and new life. It is also a time for spring cleaning—unless, of course, you are a procrastinator! You know (or may be) the kind of person I'm talking about. Procrastinators put off doing things until the last possible minute. Instead of taking care of life's little details as they come up, they "stuff" things into their "I'll do it later closet." The size of this closet is often unknown so you never know how much you can *really* cram in it. The excuse for throwing more into the closet than you take care of each day is, "I'll have time later, I'll be able to do it better later, this can wait until tomorrow." Unfortunately, tomorrow *does* finally arrive. The procrastinators walk up to their closet with "one more item" that can wait and when they open the door, *everything* comes crashing to the floor! This stockpile of "unmanaged issues" is so big it overwhelms the person who created it. "Gee! Where do I even start!? I guess I'll just cram it all back in and use another closet." Let's apply this idea to a real life example and see what can happen.

SILENCE IS NOT GOLDEN

Bill and Karen (not their real names) had been married 20 years when they came to see me. Both quiet people, each kept feelings and needs to themselves. They rarely discussed personal issues with each other, and over the years became more and more distant. Karen's main complaint was Bill's alcoholism: Bill was a drinker when Karen met him but she thought "surely he'll change, especially once we get married and have children." She never voiced her concerns about Bill's drinking, and resentment continued to build. Six children and 20 years later Karen announced that she wanted a divorce. By this time Bill had been sober for 2 years. He was stunned and stated, "I never even knew she was unhappy—she never told me my drinking bothered her. Besides, I haven't had a drink in 2 years!" This comment brought forth a stream of complaints from Karen, "Oh come on Bill, what do you think all those nights when I went to bed early were about? Why do you think I got quiet and never talked to you when you were drinking? Surely after all those years you could figure out that your drinking was making me miserable. And yeah, you stopped drinking but do you think that makes up for all the bad things that happened when you *were* drinking!?" Bill, still in shock, stated, "For God's sake, why didn't you ever tell me? I can't change the past, what do you want me to do?" Karen's reply, "I really didn't think it would matter so I decided it was better for the kids if I just kept quiet. At this point, I really don't know if there is anything you can do."

This is an excellent example of the damage "stuffed anger" creates in relationships. The desire to "avoid rocking the boat" and "protect the children" led Karen to silently carry her burden of anger until, after 20 years, it was simply too heavy to carry. There is no guarantee that if Karen had shared her feelings and concerns early on that Bill would have responded; however, her failure to share feelings and needs was a guarantee that things would remain as they were.

Working with this couple was a long, slow process. Their first task was learning to identify feelings and thoughts *as they happened* rather than their old way of avoiding issues or "waiting for the right time" (which never came). Their second task was rebuilding trust and beginning to correct years of neglect their marriage had endured. Bill and Karen participated in counseling with other couples having similar problems. After a year of therapy the marriage was greatly improved and both felt hopeful that they would not only remain married but become best friends as they had been in the early days of their marriage. Wouldn't it have been easier to prevent than correct this situation? Keep this in mind as you read this chapter and relate it to your own personal relationships!

Let's look at another example to help explain the role resentments play in creating and continuing the anger–relapse cycle. I love pearls and never thought much about *why* oysters make them, until traveling to Broome, Australia, last year. This beautiful beach town on the Western coast of Australia is one of the pearl farming capitals of the world. In Broome I learned that pearl farmers put "plastic buttons" inside oysters' shells which irritate sensitive tissues. In response, the oysters gradually "coat" these objects with what later become pearls. This natural process allows oysters to get rid of sources of irritation (foreign objects inside their shells). An added bonus is the creation of beautiful pearls.

Unfortunately, humans do not have built in mechanisms for coping with irritating experiences. Attempts to ignore the negative feelings and thoughts often fail and efforts to escape with alcohol, drugs, sleep, or food only make matters worse. Since we cannot build a protective coating around our resentments, a healthy alternative is to identify their source ("How does this relate to the patches on my quilt?"), our reactions (changes in how we think and feel), and steps we can take to resolve or reduce negative responses. The rest of this chapter will explore the basic types of resentment, discuss how resentments affect the anger–relapse cycle, and introduce tools to interrupt this destructive process (refer to Worksheet 7 for a practice exercise on redirecting resentments).

SELF-DIRECTED RESENTMENT

Resentment, like ice cream, comes in several flavors: self-directed, other directed, and directed toward you by others. Identifying primary ingredients in each type of resentment is the first step in neutralizing their toxic effect on recovery. Let's begin by exploring the most common yet least recognized form of resentment: self-directed. This type of resentment is activated by unspoken feelings, unmet needs, regrets about past experiences, and a tendency to focus on personal weaknesses and mistakes. Individuals caught in this process often think, "If I had known then what I know now I *would have* chosen a different path." Since nobody can see into the future or undo the past, each of us makes what we think are "best choices" at particular points in life. Focusing on what *might have been* is like closing the barn door *after* the horse has already run away. This unrealistic, past-focused thinking only serves to increase the danger of relapse.

Successfully avoiding self-directed resentment requires us to consider several critical factors: the condition of our self-esteem, our ability to use past experiences as tools for recovery rather than excuses for relapse, the consequences of past experiences, and the benefits of holding on to self-resentments. A closer look at each of these factors demonstrates why this type of resentment is so deadly to recovery.

Self-Esteem

As discussed in previous chapters, individuals with substance abuse disorders usually have damaged self-esteem. Years of poor choices, negative consequences, and the belief that it is "way too late" to change creates a dangerously low opinion of the self. Each time we are confronted with reminders of past events, an internal movie projector replays painful, humiliating memories. If we are unable to put these memories in proper perspective, they become excuses for further substance abuse. After all, past experience "taught us" that we've screwed up so many times that it's too late to change—so, might as well dull the pain while waiting for the end to come—*right*? (*NOT*)!

View of Past Events

Our beliefs about past events make up a second ingredient in self-directed resentment. If we identify mistakes as learning experiences it prepares us to look at what was, what is, and what is desired in the future. From this position mistakes are viewed as opportunities to develop other ways to solve problems. This positive use of past experiences moves us toward recovery. On the other hand, if we view mistakes as evidence of our unworthiness (how bad we are, how wrong we were), it fuels further episodes of alcohol or drug use.

Consequences to Self and Others

Our ability to successfully identify and defeat self-resentments is linked to consequences the source of our resentment created for self and others. The greater the negative consequences, the more difficult it is to overcome self-directed resentments. For example, if I lose my job, receive a driving while intoxicated (DWI) charge, or disrupt my marriage, the consequences are not pleasant but will not lead to death or disability to myself or others. If, however, I kill someone while driving drunk, give an innocent party the HIV virus, or cause others great personal injury or harm, my ability to resolve self-resentments will be more challenging (notice I did *not* say impossible)!

Benefits of Maintaining Self-Resentments

I can hear you now: "Jo! Are you crazy? Who gets anything out of hating themselves?" Let me give you a new way of looking at this. If I can stay focused on how bad I have been, how terrible my life has turned out, how hopeless my cause is, it allows me to avoid taking personal responsibility for my current and future behavior. If I use my addiction as an excuse for inappropriate behavior (I was drunk/high so didn't know what I was doing) I can minimize the negative consequences of my behavior. If I moan and groan about what addiction has done to my life, I can attract enablers to make excuses for me and meet my needs so I can continue my addiction. Get the picture? If you get (or get out of) more than you lose from continuing your current pattern of behavior, *why* would you change? If, however, the cost exceeds the gain, you will more seriously consider your need to identify alternative response choices.

At this point we have all the ingredients to make a self-resentment driven relapse: unspoken feelings + unmet needs + regrets about past experiences + the tendency to focus on our weaknesses and mistakes + poor self-esteem + the belief that mistakes justify further substance abuse + negative consequences of past behavior for self and others + the benefits we gain from holding onto self-resentments. This is quite a recipe, wouldn't you agree? So, if it takes so much trouble to make it, might we choose to make something else instead? "How do we do that Jo, this sounds hard!" Well folks, it *is* hard! Recovery takes a lot of time and energy. Another way to look at this is to consider how much time, energy, and pain your *current* behavior is costing you. I guarantee you that in the long run, learning to release self-resentments (remembering but letting go) will consume much less energy than holding on to your current responses. Releasing self-resentments also increases the likelihood you will achieve quality sobriety, discover positive aspects of your self, and create opportunities for personal growth and intimacy with others. So, you say, "How do we begin this awesome journey?" The steps below provide a starting point for recovery. Remember: The more you challenge old behavior and thinking, the more skilled you will become in applying healthy alternatives.

Beginning Steps for Overcoming Self-Directed Resentments

1. *Identify triggers* that activate self-directed resentments. When you find yourself thinking the worst, take a time-out! Get out your journal and write down your thoughts. Consider where you were immediately before a self-resentment reared its ugly head. What were you doing, who was with you, what was going on around you? How does the current self-resentment connect with the patches on your quilt (old messages about your negative qualities or worthlessness)? Learning to identify self-resentment triggers is the first step in turning them around.

2. *Look for feelings behind the mask.* Self-directed resentments come in handy when you want to avoid feelings. By focusing on your mistakes and how bad you have been/still are, you can use anger to cover up more painful feelings like sadness, fear, confusion, inadequacy, loneliness, and guilt. Although self-resentments disguise deeper emotions, these emotions will continue to surface until you address them. A word of warning, when strong emotions are "swallowed" they generally find ways of dramatically popping up at the most inopportune times! For what it's worth, just know that it takes less energy to cry than to beat ourselves up. The reason we choose the latter is because we don't know how or are scared to express sadness or fear.

3. *Develop action plans to redirect self-directed resentments.* Since we cannot go back and alter past events, what wisdom has been gained from painful life choices? When self-directed resentments threaten to send you back into former patterns of destructive behavior, take a time-out, challenge self-defeating behaviors, practice problem solving, call a friend, use a stress management exercise, do *anything* to interrupt this process *before* it leads you into an ambush! The key lies in advance planning. *Always* have a primary plan and several alternatives to increase the potential of a successful outcome when confronted with high-risk situations (events that tempt you to misdirected anger and/or use of substances). Think badger! These rodents *always* have several avenues of escape to safeguard the survival of their species. If a badger can do it so can you!

4. *Work on self-forgiveness.* This does not mean "forget it and move on" (an unrealistic ideal). Self-forgiveness (the realistic alternative) involves remembering the source of a particular self-resentment, grieving the losses it created for self and others, making amends when possible, identifying lessons learned from the experience, taking responsibility for past actions, and then putting all this in perspective (generating a file in your mind to store this information in a minimized status) so it has less effect on current and future events.

5. *Allow time for this to happen!* The art of self-forgiveness is just that, an art. It is a process that develops slowly across time and requires ongoing patience and commitment. Nothing this important comes easy so realize you are not cleaning out a closet, you are building a new home without benefit of a full set of blueprints! When you find yourself feeling impatient or unhappy during this process, ask yourself the following questions:

    a. What price should I pay for my mistake?
    b. How much and how long do I have to pay for being human?
    c. When will the debt be paid in full?

I promise you self-imposed penalties are more severe than any sentence others might impose. If you have suffered at your own hands for more than a day, go back through this list and identify what factors are feeding your self-directed resentment. Ask yourself one final question: "If I spend the next day, week, month, year, years punishing myself, will it change the outcome of my mistake?" If the answer is no, look at the benefits you are getting from holding on to your self-directed resentment—it may be costing you more than it's worth!

OTHER DIRECTED RESENTMENT

The anger–relapse cycle is also affected by a second type of resentment: those we hold against others. Like self-directed resentment, other directed resentment is created by unspoken feelings, unmet needs, and regrets involving past experiences. The major difference is our energies are focused on the weaknesses and mistakes of others rather than our own. Other directed resentments arise when we believe others have *deliberately* ignored our feelings or *purposefully* neglected our needs.

Although on the surface it seems quite reasonable to hold others responsible for ignoring the obvious, in reality, we rarely identify feelings and needs openly so others will know they exist! Most people go through life with the unrealistic belief that others (especially those to whom we are close) *automatically* know what we are thinking, feeling, and needing. This magical thinking prevents us from identifying wants and needs to others which sets us (and them) up for resentment. My husband and I, both clinical social workers, have 29 years of combined practice experience. This should mean we are *really* good at reading minds (*right!*). How successful do you think *we* are at reading *each other's* minds (I promise you we blunder as badly as everyone else)! If you don't say it, assume others don't know. My motto is, "The only mind I can read is my own and even then it's touch and go!"

The tendency to focus on past events rather than current experiences also fuels other directed resentment. We blame, shame, fault find, point out weaknesses, overlook strengths, criticize, compare, threaten, and do all sorts of things to let others know just how wrong they were/are/will always be (all without ever saying why we are so upset)! Other focused resentments remind me of the movie *Mr. Mom*. During one scene he loaded the washing machine with about four loads of clothes and enough soap to wash for an army. He just kept putting in more and more and more. Once the washer was running, the pressure from this abuse caused the machine to rip its hoses out of the wall and "walk" across the basement. This was one of the funniest scenes in the movie. However, when we treat real people the way Mr. Mom treated that washing machine it is *anything* but funny.

Applying other directed resentments to this example, we start out feeling ignored or otherwise unappreciated with someone in our life. Rather than openly stating the source of our distress, we blame, shame, ridicule, ignore, threaten, or punish others for mistakes they are not even aware of (because we never told them). As this process continues, we stuff more and more and more of our true feelings inside getting angrier and angrier because the other person hasn't figured out why we are mad. At first, the person witnessing this behavior feels confused and puzzled. As the abuse continues, the other person experiences hurt feelings and unmet needs. When everyone finally reaches overload they let each other have it (usually with no clear understanding of what even started the disagreement)! The resulting cold war or firefight creates another event that each adds to their "resentment armory" for the next battle.

Anyone reading this can see that other directed resentment creates a great deal of pain for everyone involved. Since it is so negative, why do we hold onto it? Well, as with self-directed resentment, a number of ingredients (very similar to the original recipe) go into creating an other directed resentment relapse: unspoken feelings + unmet needs + regrets about past experiences + focusing on the mistakes and weaknesses of others + poor self-esteem + our view of the past + consequences to self and others + the nature of our relationship with the "offending party" + benefits from maintaining other directed resentments. A brief review of these ingredients will illustrate the equally damaging result of other directed resentments.

Unspoken Feelings/Unmet Needs

We fail to identify our current thoughts, feelings, and needs, then blame others for not figuring it out! If we don't give people an opportunity to identify and respond to our feelings and needs, it seems rather unfair to hold them responsible—doesn't it?!

Regrets about the Past

The past is gone but not forgotten! Holding the past against someone is about as fair as asking a 70-year-old person to compete in a beauty contest with 20-year-olds. They may still look great, but in this culture the belief that youth equals beauty would doom them to failure! Past-driven regrets fuel resentment which in turns ignites the anger–relapse cycle.

Focusing on Others' Weaknesses and Mistakes

Well, well, if I spend all my energy pointing out *your* flaws, guess what I can avoid doing? Enough said!

Poor Self-Esteem

Gee, if I don't like me very much and I focus on your flaws, I can feel a little better about me—at least for a little while.

Our View of the Past

Wouldn't it be wonderful if we could use past misunderstandings as a way to strengthen relationships rather than bash each other over the head? I had an opportunity to do this when my sister died 6 years ago. My best friend did not come to the viewing or funeral and I was very hurt. Instead of stuffing this hurt and allowing it to turn into a resentment, I told her how hurt I was and how much I had needed her support. She had not realized this loss had affected me so deeply and apologized with tenderness and regret. This event made us closer and I bet she'll be there for me no matter who or what dies in the future! Try using past experiences to strengthen your bridges rather than to burn them down.

Consequences to Self and Others

When the actions of others create "embarrassing moments" we tend to be less forgiving. When someone says or does something that creates serious and/or lasting negative consequences (especially if there were witnesses) it is difficult to address resentments and let it go. The rule of thumb is the more public the event and the more serious the negative consequences, the more difficult is forgiveness (notice I never said it is impossible)!

The Nature of Your Relationship to the "Offending Party"

Whether you are well-known partners, friends, coworkers, or strangers plays a role in other directed resentments as does the condition of your relationship with the "offending party." In general, the more personal the relationship, the greater the risk for other directed resentment *unless* you openly share and resolve issues as they occur (as I did with my friend). A second factor involves the condition of the relationship. Just as a fence with one missing board is easier to repair than a fence with an entire section missing, relationships in good repair are more easily mended than relationships filled with conflict.

The Benefit of Maintaining Other Directed Resentments

Keeping it short and sweet, again, if I am busy looking at your short-comings, I can avoid looking at mine—at least for now.

Obviously other directed resentment is every bit as painful as self-directed resentment. Having identified the ingredients that go into creating this behavior, what steps can be taken to defuse it? What if the other person refuses to cooperate? How can resentments toward strangers be resolved to avoid poisoning ourselves and others with misdirected anger? The next section will shed some light on these questions.

Beginning Steps for Overcoming Other Directed Resentments

1. *Tell it like it is.* Be sure you clearly identify what it is you are upset about. *We* know what we are thinking, but others often need very specific feedback before they *really* understand our distress. Since it is easy to overlap issues, use time-out to identify areas of concern and approach them one at a time. Nothing creates resentments faster than overloading others with a whole list of complaints all at once! Be clear what you want or need and be equally clear about what you don't want or need. Use the problem-solving model to help you successfully navigate this process. Remember to focus on the problem *not* who is to blame!

2. *Redirect that self-talk!* Other directed resentments *love* nothing better than negative self-talk. All those nasty little messages about the other person's shortcomings produce the same effect as kerosene on a campfire. Pay attention to your self-talk and redirect it when it becomes blaming or shaming. Yes, I hear you: "But Jo, what if I really am right and they won't even listen to me?" Remember the goal of this book is to teach you how to redirect your own behavior *regardless of what everybody else does!* State your opinion using "I" messages, ask

for what you want and set limits you can live with. This will increase the chance that others will cooperate, but it is no guarantee—especially when strangers, active substance abusers, very angry or mentally ill people are involved. When you can't get cooperation, the goal becomes maintaining control of your own behavior no matter what. The long-term pleasure from yelling, hitting, or using drugs and alcohol is simply not worth the short-term "warm fuzzies" you get from acting out! If you still think it's worth it, reread this book or come to Texas and participate in my anger management/relapse prevention training program!

3. *Reframe the resentment.* This is just a fancy way of saying change the way you think about what happened. Consider the other person's point of view (yes they do have one)! When I work with very aggressive individuals who yell, curse, and threaten, I remind myself that no one acts that way unless they feel insecure and out of control. People act out in all kinds of ways but the bottom line is all this strutting and feather spreading is an attempt to create the illusion of being in control! Avoid the temptation to take it personally—nine times out of ten it's not about you, it's about *them.* I know this is very hard and I agree! Once again, the goal of this book is not to make life easy, it is to direct response choices so you have the highest potential for achieving and maintaining quality sobriety.

4. *Strive to let go of the past.* Again, easier said than done! Remember that the only one you hurt by remaining focused on the past is yourself! If my spouse divorces me and 20 years later I'm still bitter and alone, who is suffering, them or me? Better to get professional counseling and allow my friends to help me through the grieving process so I can move on and find happiness elsewhere. If I make a bad choice when buying a car and spend every day beating myself up for the mistake, is it helping or hurting me? Better to use this as a learning experience. Next time I buy a new car, I'll *know* how to get the best deal! If the person I resent is a stranger and I cannot share my resentment with them directly will replaying all the ways I can get even help me or hurt me? A better way to handle it is to change my thinking, talk to a friend, work out to get rid of my tension. If after these examples you *still* elect to hold onto the past, look at what you are getting out of it and weigh any potential benefits against what it's costing you—you'll be surprised how much you're losing!!

RESENTMENTS OTHERS DIRECT TOWARD US

The third type of resentment that affects the anger–relapse cycle is resentments others direct toward us. This is the most difficult resentment to manage because we cannot make others let go of their resentments toward us. People carry resentments against others for all the reasons identified above: Their self-esteem is poor so they have to bash others in order to feel powerful. They are past focused and don't know how to remember and let go. They have experienced pain or embarrassment at our hand (whether intentional or accidental) and refuse to forgive us for past behavior. Our relationship with them is strained or no longer exists and they have not resolved their issues and moved on. They get to feel right by making us wrong. They use others to avoid openly expressing feelings or needs. They focus on our weak points to avoid having to identify and acknowledge their own. The list goes on and on.

Successfully managing resentments directed toward us by others, like taking a kayak through rapids, requires a high degree of self-control and skill. These qualities can only be acquired by *repeatedly* applying coping skills identified in this book. It is a very difficult process and you may often think, "Why bother, they asked for it, so I'll let them have it." Before acting on this impulse ask yourself, "Is it worth reducing myself to their level?" "It is worth risking my sobriety to get even?" "What long-term benefits will I gain from playing into their destructive behavior?" If all else fails, call someone who loves you and have them let you role-play what you *wish* you could say to the person attacking you but are choosing not to so negative consequences can be avoided. The following guidelines introduce the concept of defensive resentment dodging.

Beginning Steps for Overcoming Resentments Others Hold Against You

1. *Remain calm and nondefensive.* "Yeah, right Jo!" It is *very* difficult to avoid becoming defensive when others are slinging negative comments in your direction. Your top priority is to challenge the desire to take it personally. Remember others only become aggressive when they feel threatened, and what you are seeing is really a reflection of the other person's distress. Apply positive self-talk and avoid feeding into negative comments meant to "hook you" into unnecessary conflicts. Body language is also important. Avoid direct eye contact, remain at a comfortable distance (even if you have to apply time-out and leave the scene), keep verbal responses to a minimum, and when you do speak, use a low, calm tone of voice. This is basic strategy for defusing anger and it works—if *you* will apply it! Remember, you are *only* responsible for your own responses *not* what the other person is doing. By controlling *your* behavior you can have a significant impact on the outcome. I have used this technique many times with raging clients and avoided physical injuries on at least three occasions. Had I allowed my desire to verbally "attack back" get the better of me, I could have been seriously injured. Remember the goal is to minimize negative consequences for everyone involved, if possible, and for yourself if your attempts to defuse others' anger fail.

    2. *Make amends, when possible.* This refers primarily to ongoing relationships; however, there are times when offering amends to strangers and acquaintances is both possible and helpful. If you get short-tempered with a grocery store clerk on a bad day, it never hurts to apologize after the fact. It's good practice and that clerk will remember you in a positive way the next time you come in. If you make a hostile comment to your neighbor when their dog "makes" in your bushes *again*, take a time-out, use detouring self-talk and problem solving, then go to them using "I" messages and try to work it out. You may be pleasantly surprised, and if not, what have you lost? If you yell at your child and feel guilty later, apologize (not for your anger which may have been justified, but for the way you delivered it). Modeling this kind of behavior is the most powerful influence you can have on others' behavior. I never teach what I am not willing to do myself for this very reason.

    By now you're probably thinking, "This is all well and good when others' cooperate, but what if they don't?" Your *only* responsibility is to *offer* amends, you cannot make another person accept them. Accept responsibility for your actions, offer to correct the situation if possible, and if you cannot make amends, offer an apology. If the other person refuses to accept your apology, remember that you cannot alter the past nor change their current feelings about your past behavior. Maintain a nondefensive attitude and let it go. Once you have offered amends, you are free to move on to current issues and set goals for the future.

3. *Continue moving forward with your own recovery* regardless of whether you are successful in resolving resentments others hold against you. You can best influence others by replacing former patterns of self-defeating thoughts and behavior with more constructive alternatives. Although we cannot change others' thinking and behavior, changes in our own response choices often create positive change in others. The best possible outcome is that others will gradually "come around." The worst possible outcome is that others will hold onto resentments and you may have to end relationships that threaten your sobriety. No matter what happens, focus on the present and the future: The rewards that come from remembering and letting go far outweigh the benefits of getting even!

I am painfully aware of your doubt as I complete this chapter. It is hard to believe that life-long patterns of feeling, thinking, and behaving can change. Every attempt to apply a skill identified in this book requires you to challenge the possibility that others will use these changes against you, that it won't work or will make things worse, that it takes too much energy or patience to apply these skills. The only response I have is that I practice what I teach and it works 95% of the time. The other 5% I still resort to anger outbursts so I continue to teach and apply that which I am struggling to learn! These skills require constant practice but take much less energy than trying to undo all the damage misdirected anger and relapse create (see Worksheet 7 for your first practice session)! The following chapter provides suggestions for strengthening your new skills and examples to give you the courage to keep working toward the quality recovery you want and deserve.

WORKSHEET 7

ASSESSING PERSONAL RESENTMENTS

This worksheet is designed to help you identify and work through personal resentments affecting your recovery. Please answer the following questions to the best of your ability, referring back to material presented in the chapter as needed. Use one practice worksheet for each resentment and remember resentments can be self- or other directed or involve resentments others hold against you.

1. What is your greatest personal resentment? _____
    _____
    _____

2. What person(s) does this resentment involve? _____
    _____
    _____

3. How long have you held this resentment? _____
    _____
    _____

4. Have you ever attempted to resolve it?   YES _____   NO _____
    If yes, how? _____
    _____
    _____

Worksheet 7 (continued)

5. If the resentment is unresolved, what negative consequences has it created? _____

_____

6. What benefits do you get out of holding onto it? _____

_____

7. Having read this chapter and completed this worksheet, what else might you do to resolve your resentment? _____

_____

From *Anger and addiction: Breaking the relapse cycle*, by J. Clancy, 1996. Madison, CT: Psychosocial Press, pp. 186–187.

Part 3

Learning How to Fly

13

When You Roller-Skate You Get Skinned Knees

When I was a child, learning to roller-skate was a painful experience. We didn't wear knee pads back then and in the beginning I spent more time on my knees than on my feet! Since my love of skating was stronger than the pain of skinned knees, after falling I would clean my wounds and keep on skating. As time passed I fell less often and could skillfully stop, turn corners, and control my speed. I got so confident that I "forgot" how painful my early experiences had been—until I attempted ice skating. Once again I was faced with the reality that in order to develop skill in a new activity, I had to be willing to get skinned knees (or in this case, a cold bottom)! This is true for us all. Developing skill in any activity requires us to go through a process of trial and error. We try, make adjustments, try again, and finally, if we keep trying, develop some level of skill. The goal of this chapter is to convince you that the anger management/relapse prevention model *can* work, *if* you are willing to put up with a few skinned knees!

Learning to apply the anger management/relapse prevention model requires us to challenge well-known patterns of behavior. Although other response choices might create more positive results, change means we must venture into uncharted waters. I have been teaching the anger management/relapse prevention model for 7 years and have identified five basic reasons why people resist change even when their current behavior leads to negative consequences. Let's identify and explore these roadblocks to change.

1. We assume we are experts, therefore, see no need to change.
2. We are afraid of the unknown.
3. We believe change will be too hard.
4. We don't believe change is possible.
5. We assume that change cancels out everything we have done during our lives up to that point.

WE ASSUME WE ARE EXPERTS, THEREFORE, SEE NO NEED TO CHANGE

When I was 12 I *finally* convinced my parents to let me buy a horse. I had read every book I could find on owning a horse and was confident I "knew it all." The first day I owned my mare, I attempted to clean her hooves. The book said to go around the horse from foot to foot and clean the hooves with a hoof pick. I picked up the hoof pick and approached my new mare. Well, she certainly had not read the same book I had and before I cleaned even one hoof she kicked me across the stall with both back feet! Needless to say I was stunned. After all, I did *exactly* what the book said so why did I get kicked!? What the book did *not* say was that you should tie the horse's head before beginning this process to reduce the risk of getting kicked! I also failed to tell her of what I was doing (especially important since she did not yet know me and was nervous). Misty quickly taught me how much I did *not* know about horse care!

A second lesson I learned straight from the horse was how *not to* ride a newly saddle broken horse. When I bought my mare she was "green broke" which means she had only recently been trained to wear a saddle and bridle and was still nervous about carrying a rider. Instead of getting on in a pen where I would have control, I took her into an open pasture. When I put my foot in the stirrup she took off at a dead run! I went up, over, and off—landing with a crash. She stopped, turned her head, and laughed at me! I can still see the expression on her face which seemed to say, "You just *think* you know what you're doing—pay attention and I'll teach *you* a thing or two!"

A third lesson I learned the hard way was how to read "horse cues." Horses move their ears and other body parts to let each other know how they are feeling. Ears that are laid flat back mean "look out!" Forward ears and an extended muzzle mean, "Let's be friends" or "I'm curious." Before I learned this lesson I made the mistake of walking into a group of horses where my mare was standing. Little did I know the mood of this group of mares was hostile (an eligible stallion was nearby)! Had I known to pay attention to the horses' body cues, I could have avoided being kicked across the field yet again!

So how does this apply to the anger management/relapse prevention model? Well, we all "know" how to respond to events in our lives. Unfortunately, we often make situations worse by failing to pay attention to "cues" that indicate how we and others are feeling and the "triggers" that activate our reactions. The outcome, like my early experiences with Misty demonstrate, do not always pan out the way we had imagined. No matter how smart you are, how much you have read, how many life experiences you have lived through, you can *always* benefit from learning alternative response choices. Using this model, like learning to be a good horse owner, requires ongoing effort and a willingness to learn new skills as you go along. Yes, you *can* keep right on doing things just as you always have; however, if you do be sure to ask yourself "*why* am I choosing to kick and be kicked instead of learning more productive ways of managing my behavior?" You might be surprised by the answer!

WE ARE AFRAID OF THE UNKNOWN

This is especially true for chemically dependent individuals since the basic rules "don't talk, trust, or feel" make change a very frightening experience. A common thought is: "I know my current response choices create negative results but at least they're expected. What if I change and things get even worse?" People in this position rarely consider the alternative—things could get better! Maintaining an all or nothing position just makes things worse. "If I change, I have to change it *all* and *right now*!" A more practical way to approach change is one step at a time. The following examples may help you develop a more realistic attitude about approaching the unknown as it applies to change.

Think of a box turtle. When frightened, this little creature can snap its shell shut so tightly that no body parts are exposed to enemy attack. Although this is an excellent defense, the turtle could not survive if it stayed tightly closed at all times! It has many options, depending on how safe or threatened it feels: It can snap itself shut completely, open the front of its shell just enough to see, stick out its head and front legs, put all four feet out so it can walk, and so forth. These options allow the turtle to *gradually* experience its surroundings. Certainly, just as we would not expect the turtle to remain tightly shut at all times, no one would expect the turtle to be fully extended no matter what. In order to survive, the turtle must "learn" when and where it is safe enough to come out and when and where it must keep itself tightly closed to prevent harm.

Well, don't you think people are at least as smart as turtles? People, like turtles, must carefully choose when, where, how, and with whom to be open (share feelings and needs), and when, where, how, and with whom to remain closed (limit sharing of feelings and needs). This skill is developed gradually and requires time and patience. You do not have to and should not fully expose yourself to everyone, especially in situations involving acquaintances and strangers. You should, however, be able to share feelings and needs with your partner and close friends. As you begin the process of change, start off slow to avoid scaring yourself back into old patterns of behavior. Remember the story of the tortoise and the hare: Slow and steady wins the race!

A second way to introduce change into your life without activating a terror response is to approach it much like you would eat an artichoke. The best part of this vegetable is the heart, and you must patiently and carefully dismantle this vegetable leaf by leaf to reach it. Although eating an artichoke takes effort, I have never regretted it since the heart is so delicious! Changing long-standing patterns of behavior is much the same. Instead of ripping off all the layers of protection you spent years developing, gradually peel off a layer at a time, as you feel comfortable. As you make new discoveries about yourself and your circumstances, the next layer can be removed until you reach the core of who you are. Remember, you did not get where you are in a day so be patient—it will take a long time to get to the heart of what you have guarded so closely for so long. As with the artichoke, once you get there the reward will be worth the effort.

WE BELIEVE CHANGE WILL BE TOO HARD

Change *is* hard so I won't try and convince you otherwise. What you may not have considered is that staying the same is also hard, especially once negative consequences for thinking and behaving in unproductive ways start piling up. Change, when successful, is a gradual process. Like building a puzzle, change is completed in stages and the final product may not be realized for months or years. Many people become frustrated when efforts to change are not *immediately* rewarded. We resist the painful reality that current patterns of behavior have existed for years, therefore, it will take awhile to generate noticeable changes! If we are patient, and believe, change can and does occur. Let's look at an example to illustrate this point.

I have always been a tomboy. I climbed trees when my girl friends played house. They had dolls, I had model horses. They wore dresses and makeup, I wore jeans and went natural. This all worked well and good until I was nearing the end of my graduate education in social work. One of my instructors remarked, "Jo, once you're a professional you have a certain image to uphold. Dresses and makeup are an important part of presenting a professional image to your clients." Well, as you can imagine, this comment tapped into my insecurity and I responded, "Well, if my skills don't speak for themselves, I guess I won't be a very good social worker. I'm not changing who I am just to meet some imaginary guideline!" I did begin to wear dresses and pantsuits, however, but I resisted wearing makeup. I put all my energies into being the best social worker possible.

About a year into my career I met my "dream man" who happened to be on the social work staff where I worked. We developed a friendship and often shared our coffee breaks. One day we were talking about people and appearances and he casually remarked, "Jo, you have such pretty eyes, makeup sure would show them off." This casual comment forever changed my belief about makeup, and indeed, myself! First, I felt hurt and confused, "Maybe he really doesn't like me." Later, I became angry and thought, "Well, if he can't accept me the way I am, the hell with him!" As I shared my reactions with a friend, she asked me why I was so against makeup since it is so common in American culture. I had to really think about that one! What I realized is that my sisters, both much older than I, left home before I was old enough to wear makeup. I was shy so I never asked my friends to help me. Ignoring my true feelings (I felt foolish and inadequate) I reasoned that I did not want to "paint my face" anyway.

My friend offered to teach me to wear makeup. At first I said, "It'll be too hard, I'm too old (I was 30), I can't afford it, I have allergies." After a time I agreed to try and she began teaching me the art of using makeup. After a number of false starts and awkward attempts, I got pretty good at matching colors and getting a smooth, polished look. Even I had to admit it improved my appearance and hadn't changed who I was (I was still Jo on the inside, just a little more polished on the outside)!

In the beginning this shift from "natural" to "painted" was very threatening and created a lot of self-doubt and fear. My gradual shift to feeling comfortable with makeup was so subtle that I did not notice how much it had become a part of my routine until my oldest friend laughed at me for wearing waterproof mascara when we went water skiing. What had at first seemed impossible became as natural as breathing. I promise you the anger management/relapse prevention model produces a similar result. In the beginning you will feel clumsy and foolish, but if you keep practicing, it will become as natural to you as putting on makeup is for me now.

WE DON'T BELIEVE CHANGE IS POSSIBLE

I have always been an optimist, and even as a child regularly took on what others said were impossible tasks. When I was 8 years old I found a baby sparrow that had fallen from its nest. It had a few feathers but was too young to survive without its mother. I carefully placed it back in the nest, hoping its mother would reclaim it. The next day I checked the nest and realized it had been abandoned. Knowing the bird would die if I did not step in, I boldly clutched it to my chest, determined to save its tiny life. Everyone warned me that it would die, that it would never be able to live a normal life, that I would never be able to meet its need for mothering. I ignored these comments and began feeding my new baby a mixture of bread and milk with an eyedropper. I named the bird "Spunky Rosebud" because it seemed so feisty and I thought it was a girl.

I never knew how demanding a baby bird could be! It cried constantly and had to be fed every few hours. As it grew, I added worms to its diet and began showing it how to scratch and peck for food (I'm sure I looked mighty silly, but it worked)! Once Spunky Rosebud had all her feathers, I began gently tossing her into the air so she could learn to fly. She would flap her wings and land in my hand. Day after day we practiced and one day I tossed her into the air and she flew away. I was both excited and sad. Several days went by and I hoped Spunky Rosebud had found her place in the wild. Then, I heard a scratching outside the door and there was Spunky Rosebud—home for a visit! She visited off and on all summer and finally stopped coming (I assumed she found a mate and flew away). Had I believed what others told me (it's too hard, it won't work, you can't do it) this tiny, helpless bird would have died. Instead, she grew up to be strong, happy, and free.

If we believe change is possible we create the circumstances to encourage it. If we believe change is impossible we create obstacles to keep it from happening. Remember from earlier chapters that our beliefs are as powerful as the reality around us. Had people not believed that change is possible Columbus would have never discovered America, people of color would still be slaves, women would not have the right to vote, and space travel would be something that only exists in comic books. Change, if initiated in tiny stages, *is* possible! I cannot change the tide of an ocean but I sure can create ripples in a pond! Behavior change is a slow, tiring process but the end results: better self-image, the ability to get our needs met, more productive relationships with others, far outweigh the alternative: resisting change, refusing to believe, and continuing to barrel down the path to self-destruction and despair.

WE ASSUME THAT CHANGE CANCELS OUT OUR LIVES UP TO THAT POINT

I entered my first marriage very young and spent the next 14 years as a homemaker. I was very serious about my chosen profession and kept a clean house, cooked healthy meals, and devoted my energies to caring for my husband and young son. As time passed, I began to feel a need to further my education. Although homemaking was still important, I needed to expand my horizons. As I prepared to enroll in college a good friend cautioned me: "Think carefully before you take this step. It will forever change your life and there is no going back." Her comment unsettled me and I wondered if becoming a career person would somehow invalidate all the years I had spent at home cleaning house and raising a family. After all, I had spent a lot of my life being a homemaker and didn't want to feel it had been a waste of time. I chose to believe that even if my thinking changed, my past experiences were still important and would somehow make me a better person all the way around.

I have been a social worker for 9 years now and although my life is very different than it was 20 years ago, I still see those early years as an important part of my personal development. Being a homemaker taught me a lot about being a person and how to care for others. Getting an education and becoming a social worker have not changed "Jo" any more than makeup did. This process of personal growth simply opened up new aspects of myself that were always there but not yet understood. My young adulthood experiences are just as important as my current midlife experiences. Indeed, each phase of life adds new pieces to our puzzle. Learning to apply the anger management/relapse prevention model will not undo your past experiences; it will increase your awareness of where you have been and provide a smoother path to where you are going.

The anger management/relapse prevention model is only one piece of your recovery puzzle. I hope it will increase your awareness of how and why you respond as you do and provide alternatives to patterns of thinking and behaving that no longer work. Another important piece of your puzzle involves participating in 12-step recovery to support long-term, quality sobriety. Since clients often ask me how this model fits with 12-step philosophy, the final chapter of this book will address how these two very important pieces of the recovery puzzle join forces in the fight against relapse.

14

What About the Twelve Steps?

When I teach the anger management/relapse prevention model people always ask me whether they still need to practice 12-step recovery once they learn this new approach to relapse prevention. My answer without fail is YES! *Please remember that although the anger management/ relapse prevention training program is an important recovery tool, it complements but does not replace 12-step recovery programs!*

This final chapter addresses the relationship between these two very important pieces of your recovery plan.

Let's review the twelve steps as originally written before exploring the nature of this relationship.

THE TWELVE STEPS OF ALCOHOLICS ANONYMOUS*

1. We admitted we were powerless over alcohol—that our lives had become unmanageable.

*The Twelve Steps are reprinted with permission of Alcoholics Anonymous World Services, Inc. Permission to reprint the Twelve Steps does not mean that A.A. has reviewed or approved the contents of this publication, nor that A.A. agrees with the views expressed herein. A.A. is a program of recovery from alcoholism *only*—use of the Twelve Steps in connection with programs and activities which are patterned after A.A., but which address other problems, or in any other non-A.A. context, does not imply otherwise.

2. Came to believe that a power greater than ourselves could restore us to sanity.
3. Made a decision to turn our will and lives over to the care of God *as we understood Him.*
4. Made a searching and fearless moral inventory of ourselves.
5. Admitted to God, to ourselves, and to another human being the exact nature of our wrongs.
6. Were entirely ready to have God remove all these defects of character.
7. Humbly asked Him to remove our shortcomings.
8. Made a list of all persons we had harmed, and became willing to make amends to them all.
9. Made direct amends to such people whenever possible, except when to do so would injure them or others.
10. Continued to take personal inventory and when we were wrong promptly admitted it.
11. Sought through prayer and meditation to improve our conscious contact with God, *as we understood Him,* praying only for knowledge of His will for us and the power to carry that out.
12. Having had a spiritual awakening as the result of these steps, we tried to carry this message to alcoholics, and to practice these principles in all our affairs.

Having reviewed the Twelve Steps in their original form, let's explore them, one step at a time, as they relate to the anger management/ relapse prevention training program:

Step 1. "We admitted we were powerless over alcohol—that our lives had become unmanageable."

When applying this step to misdirected anger, keep in mind that anger, once it passes a certain point, becomes unmanageable. Indeed, I have written two books about anger and the relapse process, but if I ignore triggers and cues that alert me to increasing anger it will result in an anger outburst. The harder I try to convince myself that I am in control, the less control I have. I must admit that my power to redirect anger, much like the alcoholic's power to avoid relapse, lies in early identification of relapse triggers and rapid application of relapse prevention tools. Once my anger reaches a certain point, or I take my first drink, I become powerless to interrupt the process until it comes full circle.

Step 2. "Came to believe that a power greater than ourselves could restore us to sanity."

This means admitting that it takes more than sheer willpower to interrupt the anger–relapse connection. Since we cannot interrupt this process by will alone, we must ask for help from therapists to learn relapse prevention skills, peers to provide emotional support and guidance, family members and friends to help us initiate change and practice new behaviors, and a higher power to provide the courage needed to reach out and accept help from the individuals identified above.

Step 3. "Made a decision to turn our will and our lives over to the care of God *as we understood Him.*"

Simply stated, you have to surrender to win! If I am swimming in the ocean and a strong current sweeps me out to sea I have two choices: I can struggle and swim with all my might hoping to reach shore before weariness overcomes me and I drown, or I can swim a little, do a dead man's float, swim a little more, and gradually work my way back to safety. The first option leaves little hope for survival. The second increases the odds that I will live to tell the story another day.

This means admitting that although responsible for our actions, there are limits beyond which we have no control. When we stubbornly defend the belief that we can do it on our own without the help of anyone or anything, the result is often relapse. Learning to accept our limitations and make choices with the guidance of a higher power increases our chances of recognizing and interrupting the anger–relapse connection.

Step 4. "Made a searching and fearless moral inventory of ourselves."

When we stop looking outward and shift our focus toward our inner self, it is often surprising to see what comes into focus! Step 4 requires us to review past events so we can better understand how we build up to and fuel the anger–relapse connection. This is a difficult process which involves clearing away the fog that so often clouds our judgment. Conducting a personal inventory requires us to identify how we feel, think, behave, and to observe our surroundings when changes arise. To successfully complete our inventory we must stop blaming others for the shortcomings in our lives and channel our efforts into developing ways to redirect our own response choices—regardless of what others say or do.

Step 5 "Admitted to God, to ourselves and to another human being the exact nature of our wrongs."

This means identifying past patterns of unproductive or destructive behavior, and taking responsibility to initiate change. If we never admit our mistakes we can explain away almost anything, and will continue to resist change:
"I had to beat the hell out of my partner, he or she wouldn't shut up! They asked for it!"
"I needed that drink to calm down after what I've been through—you would have done the same thing if you were in my shoes!"
"It wasn't MY fault! If_____ hadn't done_____ I wouldn't have had to act that way!"
Identifying mistakes as an acceptable and correctable condition of the human race provides opportunities to discover strengths that can lead us to more productive response choices. When I think of step 5 in relation to the anger management/relapse prevention model the following statement comes to mind: "If nobody died and the world didn't end, it's fixable (if someone died or an event is unchangeable, the goal becomes remembering, forgiving, and letting go)." Step 5 allows us to admit that human beings (yes that means you too!) make mistakes. That when mistakes are admitted we can learn from them and, although past events cannot be changed, we *can* change the outcome of current and future events!

Step 6. "Were entirely ready to have God remove all these defects of character."

This step means coming to a position of willingness to change our uncomfortably familiar, safe patterns of behavior. This requires us to courageously identify our greatest fears and confront feelings we may have masked with substance abuse and anger for most of our lives. To risk change one must reach a point where the pain from current behavior is greater than the fear of change. Once this occurs, a sense of readiness for change allows one to fiercely confront imperfections and strive to identify and activate character strengths.

Step 7. "Humbly asked Him to remove our shortcomings."

This means asking for guidance in downplaying our shortcomings and highlighting our strengths. I truly believe that our core character remains intact, even in the presence of change, but we can identify shortcomings and develop ways to reduce their negative influence on our lives. I compare this with minimizing one computer program so you can open another. Both are running, but one dominates the screen while the second is quietly running in the corner. The goal of this model is to minimize the now dominant anger–relapse connection and maximize a more productive alternative. The "old program" is still running, but can be kept in a minimized status to reduce the risk of relapse. Pay attention to your triggers and cues—this old program can maximize itself in periods of stress unless you remember the early identification/intervention process taught throughout this book!

Step 8. "Made a list of all the persons we had harmed, and became willing to make amends to them all."

This means assuming a position of truthfulness about one's personal role in life conflicts. This step challenges us to stop blaming people, places, and things outside ourselves for past, present, and future problems. It invites us to identify those to whom we have caused pain or loss because of unproductive response choices. To accomplish this task, we must assume personal responsibility for our own thoughts, feelings, and behavior—regardless of what others think, feel, or do. Failure to accomplish this task generates resentment and refusal to even acknowledge that amends are necessary.

Step 9. "Made direct amends to such people wherever possible, except when to do so would injure them or others."

This step means making efforts to identify and address our personal response choices that damaged or destroyed relationships. As the step implies, this is not always possible; however, in many cases, taking the first step to begin repairs can lead to powerful and positive outcomes:

    A. Examples where amends are possible and may generate positive outcomes for both parties:

        Example 1: You had a fight with your older brother at a family dinner 10 years ago and have not spoken to him since. You always used the excuse, "He started it, he can apologize first!" Following step 9, you stop blaming and shaming and call your brother! This may or may not begin the process of repair, but if you don't call, you are *guaranteed* nothing will change!

        Example 2: Your friend does not come to your mother's funeral and you are deeply hurt. Rather than approaching this friend with your feelings, you write a nasty letter telling them how terrible they are and then refuse to discuss it when they respond. The belief, "If they were really my friend, they would have come without being asked" allows you to make the other person wrong and avoid dealing with your own hurt feelings. Applying step 9, you would call this friend, explain, from your viewpoint, what happened, and be willing to admit your role in the current conflict (not stating how you felt and what you needed). Again, this may or may not begin the process of relationship repair, but until you call—you'll never know!!

    B. Examples where amends are not possible but positive outcomes may still occur for oneself:

        Example 1: You are responsible for the deaths of several civilians in a combat setting. You experience guilt and great emotional pain when you think of your actions, and have used alcohol, drugs, and anger to hide your pain. The excuse is "I really screwed up, I don't deserve to live."

During the process of recovery, you discover step 9. Amends are not possible directly because the individuals involved are dead. Amends can be made indirectly. Using role-plays, letters, and other forms of therapy, you can release anger and guilt, initiate requests for forgiveness, and begin the process of remembering and letting go.

Example 2: You have lived a life of violence and substance abuse leaving a trail of broken and damaged relationships in your wake. After beginning a recovery program you identify all those to whom you would like to make amends. You realize that so much pain was generated it would do more harm than good to make contact and stir up old wounds. Again, amends cannot be made directly; however, you can make amends indirectly using letters, role-plays, and other forms of therapy. The goal is to admit your role in the process, identify more productive means of managing similar situations in the future, and initiate the process of remembering, self-forgiveness, and letting go.

Step 10. "Continued to take personal inventory and when we were wrong promptly admitted it."

This requires us to make a commitment to observe our physical reactions, feelings, thoughts, and behavior for signs of increasing relapse risk. Simply stated, this means paying attention to the subtle shifts in our mood, thinking, and behavior so we can interrupt the process before we relapse and/or make an inappropriate response choice (stuffing or exploding our anger). We must also constantly review the triggers that activate these shifts and assess whether our current coping skills are still effective. When relapse triggers are noted (we find ourselves in active relapse—with or without active substance use, or returning to former pattern of behavior—stuffing or exploding anger) we disclose this shift and take responsibility for interrupting this process. The presence of relapse triggers can be viewed from two positions: "Uh oh, I screwed up again!" or "I got caught with my pants down! What can I learn from this experience to reduce the risk of it happening again?" I, of course, wholeheartedly support the second position!

Step 11. "Sought through prayer and meditation to improve our conscious contact with God *as we understood Him*, praying only for the knowledge of His will for us and the power to carry that out."

From an anger management perspective, this means achieving a sense of balance and inner peace. Once a sense of personal direction is identified we can better apply anger management/relapse prevention tools. Time-out, much like prayer and meditation, provides opportunities to evaluate our feelings, identify options, and apply appropriate response choices. Self-talk is also an important part of this process. Taking action to redirect our thoughts in a positive direction creates a channel through which we can find inner peace. Time-out and detouring self-talk also promote patience and courage necessary to activate the recovery process. Finally, this step challenges us to stop trying to control our destiny so fiercely and trust that our lives will unfold as they should *if* we can just step out of the way!

Step 12. "Having had a spiritual awakening as the result of these Steps, we tried to carry this message to others, and to practice these principles in all our affairs."

Step 12 means taking the wisdom and knowledge developed during your training and teaching it to others. Gaining knowledge is an important part of recovery; however, it is worthless if we fail to apply it to daily life circumstances. This incomplete circuit significantly reduces the potential for long-term, quality life changes. The old saying, "You teach that which you seek to learn" is especially true here. When our level of understanding is great enough to teach others, it reinforces our ability to apply the model in our own lives. Practicing anger management/relapse prevention skills, teaching these skills to others through example, and identifying areas where improvement is still needed, brings to life the process called recovery.

As shown above, 12-step philosophy is highly compatible with the anger management/relapse prevention model. Both approaches promote the belief that as human beings we all have areas of strength and weakness. Identifying when and where we need support, assuming personal responsibility for both our actions and their consequences, and demonstrating willingness to change our behavior are critical to the recovery process. The need to *develop* and *apply* coping skills for relapse prevention are also vital to this process. Finally, having the courage to reveal our limitations, admit that we make mistakes, acknowledge that we sometimes make poor choices, and own that we *never* have *all* the "right" answers challenges us to share this knowledge with others who are a step behind us in this journey called recovery.

Epilogue

Finishing this book is significant because it marks the end of a project I began 4 years ago. In 1992 I wrote a book titled *Anger and addiction: Breaking the relapse cycle.* This book was originally written for clients. Due to my lack of experience as an author, the book was three years finding its way to a publisher and had to be rewritten for professionals, adding another year to the process. It represents a great personal achievement: my first published work. My hope is that it will guide other mental health professionals in their efforts to interrupt the anger–relapse cycle.

Although an important contribution to the professional literature, *Anger and addiction* did not meet my original goal: the creation of an anger management/relapse prevention guide for clients. *Anger and relapse: Breaking the cycle* **finally** allowed me to accomplish this goal! This book is for regular folks like me and you. I hope it is helpful and offer these final suggestions to help you get the most out of the exercises and worksheets you have completed along the way:

1. First and most important, remember that in order to interrupt existing patterns of behavior, we must first understand how they came to be. Take the exercise regarding the patches on your quilt seriously, it is the cornerstone of this process called *change*.

2. Once we understand how and why we came to develop our response choices, we must learn to recognize the triggers and cues that call them into action. Developing awareness of our personalized buildup process is critical to interruption of the anger–relapse cycle.

3. Learn as many alternative response choices as you can. You can never have too many tricks in your bag.

4. Remember to periodically evaluate your response choices to see if they are still valid. We change across time and so does the effectiveness of existing response choices (i.e., what worked at 15 may no longer be valid at 40).

5. Remember that change is a slow, painful process. It takes time and effort to bring about shifts in how we feel, think, and behave. When you feel discouraged that you are not changing as fast as you had hoped, weigh the short-term benefits of holding onto your existing response choices against the long-term benefits of replacing them with more productive alternatives. I promise you an investment that yields a high rate of return!

6. Be prepared for things to get worse before they get better. Anytime you stir the pot, it brings painful memories to the surface. The only way out is through, and it hurts more before it feels better. If you stick with it and do the grief work necessary to remember but let go of negative experiences in your past, you can free yourself to create a happier today and tomorrow.

7. Remember that the anger management/relapse prevention program is only one piece of your recovery plan. Don't discount the importance of participating in 12-step recovery to strengthen and sustain your efforts to achieve long-term, quality sobriety.

8. Others will challenge whether the changes you are demonstrating are "for real." Expect them to poke sticks at you to see if the change is real or Memorex. Consistent displays of new behavior across time is the most powerful tool in convincing others that the changes they see are the real deal. Just remember, you cannot control others' responses but you *can* control your own responses *regardless of what others say and do.*

9. Believe in yourself! I have provided you with a guide to recovery but it is only as valuable as your belief in yourself. My challenge to you is to believe, to take baby steps, and to see where you are in 5, 10, 15, and 20 years. I would have never believed 20 years ago that I would be where I am now—I guess the optimism that gave me the courage to save Spunky Rosebud is still alive and well within me!

10. Finally, if I have accomplished nothing more than to make you think about your current response choices and question why you hang onto them when they cause you such pain, then I have created a shift in your thinking that may later serve as a catalyst for change. Let me leave you with a thought that served as the catalyst in my personal growth experience: "I hope someday you see in yourself what I see in you today." Unfortunately the friend who said this to me is deceased; however, she would be amazed to see the power this comment had in re-shaping my life *once I was ready and willing to believe in myself!*

GOOD LUCK IN YOUR RECOVERY ADVENTURES!

Suggested Reading List

This book, designed to be "reader friendly," does not include technical definitions or references in the text. Some of you may want additional information on ideas and concepts introduced in the book, and the following reading list provides a starting point for further study. It is organized by chapter and topic to make locating references related to specific areas of interest easier.

CHAPTER 1

Definitions of Anger

Clancy, J. (1996). *Anger and addiction: Breaking the relapse cycle, a teaching guide for professionals.* Madison, CT: Psychosocial Press.

Fonberg, E. (1979). Physiological mechanisms of emotional and instrumental aggression. In S. Feshback & A. Fraczek (Eds.), *Aggression and behavior change: Biological and social processes* (pp. 6–53). New York: Praeger.

Green, E., & Green, E. (1979). General and specific applications of thermal feedback. In J. V. Basmajian (Ed.), *Biofeedback: Principles and practice for clinicians* (pp. 153–169). Baltimore: Williams & Williams.

MaClean, P. D. (1955). The limbic system. *Psychosomatic Medicine, 17,* 355.

Moyer, K. E. (1976). Kinds of aggression and their physiological basis. In K. E. Moyer (Ed.), *Physiology of aggression and implications for control: An anthology of readings* (pp. 1–21). New York: Raven.

Schachter, J. (1957). Pain, fear, and anger in hypertensives and normotensives. *Psychosomatic Medicine, 19*,17–29.

Spielberger, C., Jacobs, G., Russell, S., & Crane, R. S. (1983). Assessment of anger: The state-trait anger scale. In J. Butcher & C. Spielberger (Eds.), *Advances in personality assessment* (Vol. 2, pp. 161–186). Hillsdale, NJ: Lawrence Erlbaum.

Williams, R., & Williams, V. (1993). *Anger kills.* New York: Times Books.

Definitions of Addiction

Clancy, J. (1996). *Anger and addiction: Breaking the relapse cycle, a teaching guide for professionals.* Madison, CT: Psychosocial Press.

Gorski, T., & Miller, M. (1986). *Staying sober: A guide for relapse prevention.* Independence, MO: Independence Press.

Jellinek, E. M. (1960). *The disease concept of alcoholism.* New Haven, CT: Hillhouse Press.

Leiber, C. S., Hasumara, Y., Teschke, R., Matsuzaki, S., & Korsten, M. (1975). The effect of chronic ethanol consumption on acetaldehyde metabolism. In K. O. Lindros & C. J. P. Ericksson (Eds.), *The role of acetaldehyde in the actions of ethanol.* Helsinki: Finnish Foundation for Alcohol Studies.

Mello, N. K. (1972). Behavioral studies in alcoholism. In B. Kissin & H. Begleiter (Eds.), *The biology of alcoholism* (Vol. 2, pp. 219–291). New York: Plenum.

Miliam, J., & Ketcham, K. (1981). *Under the influence: A guide to the myths and realities of alcoholism.* Seattle, WA: Madrona.

Nathan, P. E., Titler, N. A., Lowenstein, L. M., Solomon, P., & Rossi, A. M. (1970). Behavioral analysis on chronic alcoholism. *Archives of General Psychiatry, 22,* 419–430.

Schuckit, M. A., Li, T. K., Cloninger, C. R., & Deitrich, R. A. (1985). The genetics of alcoholism: A summary of the conference convened at the University of California, Davis. *Alcoholism: Clinical and Experimental Research, 9*(6), 475–492.

Valliant, G. E. (1983). *The natural history of alcoholism: Causes, patterns, and paths to recovery.* Cambridge, MA: Harvard University Press.

Wallace, J. (1985). *Alcoholism: New light on the disease.* Warwick, RI: Edgehill Pubns.

Definitions of Relapse

Clancy, J. (1996). *Anger and addiction: Breaking the relapse cycle, a teaching guide for professionals.* Madison, CT: Psychosocial Press.

Daley, D. (1988). *Relapse prevention.* Bradenton, FL: Human Services Institute.

Gorski, T., & Miller, M. (1986). *Staying sober: A guide for relapse prevention.* Independence, MO: Independence Press.

CHAPTER 2

Physical Factors Involved in Anger Reactions

Leeper, R. W. (1968). The motivational theory of emotion. In M. B. Arnold (Ed.), *The nature of emotion.* Baltimore: Penguin.

MaClean, P. D. (1955). The limbic system. *Psychosomatic Medicine, 17*, 355.

Moyer, K. E. (1976). Kinds of aggression and their physiological basis. In K. E. Moyer (Ed.), *Physiology of aggression and implications for control: An anthology of readings* (pp. 1–21). New York: Raven.

Schachter, S. (1957). Pain, fear, and anger in hypertensives and normotensives. *Psychosomatic Medicine, 19*, 17–29.

Psychological and Social Factors Involved in Anger Reactions

Abramson, L., Seligman, M., & Teasdale, J. (1978). Learned helplessness in humans: Critique and reformulation. *Journal of Abnormal Psychology, 87*, 49–74.

Bandura, A. (1969). *Principles of behavior modification.* New York: Holt, Rinehart & Winston.

Bandura, A. (1971). *Psychological modeling: Conflict theories.* Chicago: Aldine-Atherton.

Bandura, A. (1977). *Social learning theory.* Englewood Cliffs, NJ: Prentice-Hall.

Bandura, A. (1986). *Social foundations of thought and action: A social–cognitive theory.* Englewood Cliffs, NJ: Prentice-Hall.

Beck, A. (1988). *Love is never enough.* New York: Harper & Row.

Black, C. & Bucky, S. (1986). Interpersonal and emotional consequences of being an adult child of an alcoholic. *International Journal of Addictions, 21*(2), 213–231.

Clancy, J. (1996). *Anger and addiction: Breaking the relapse cycle, a teaching guide for professionals.* Madison, CT: Psychosocial Press.

DiClemente, C. C. (1993). Changing addictive behaviors: A process perspective. *Current Directions in Psychological Science, 2*(4), 101–106.

Ellis, A. (1988). *How to stubbornly refuse to make yourself miserable about any-thing—Yes anything!* Secaucus, NJ: Lyle Stuart.

Ellis, A., & Becker, I. (1982). *A guide to personal happiness.* North Hollywood, CA: Wilshire.

Ellis, A., & Harper, R. A. (1975). *A guide to rational living.* North Hollywood, CA: Wilshire.

Seligman, M. (1975). *Helplessness: On depression, development, and death.* San Francisco: Freeman.

Shapiro, D. (1965). *Neurotic lifestyles.* New York: Basic Books.

Wolf, E. (1988). *Treating the self.* New York: Guilford Press.

CHAPTER 3

Learned Behavior, Addiction, and the Anger Response

Abramson, L., Seligman, M., & Teasdale, J. (1978). Learned helplessness in humans: Critique and reformulation. *Journal of Abnormal Psychology, 87*, 49–74.

204   ANGER AND RELAPSE

Annis, H., & Davis, C. (1987). Assessment of expectancies in alcohol dependent clients. In G. A. Marlatt & D. Donovan (Eds.), *Assessment of addictive behaviors* (pp. 84–111). New York: Guilford Press.

Annis, H., & Davis, C. (1987). Self-efficacy and the prevention of alcoholic relapse: Initial findings from a treatment trial. In T. Baker & D. Cannon (Eds.), *Addictive disorders: Psychological research on assessment and treatment* (pp. 88–112). New York: Praeger.

Bandura, A. (1969). *Principles of behavior modification.* New York: Holt, Rinehart & Winston.

Bandura, A. (1971). *Psychological modeling: Conflict theories.* Chicago: Aldine-Atherton.

Bandura, A. (1977). *Social learning theory.* Englewood Cliffs, NJ: Prentice-Hall.

Bandura, A. (1986). *Social foundations of thought and action: A social–cognitive theory.* Englewood Cliffs, NJ: Prentice-Hall.

Clancy, J. (1996). *Anger and addiction: Breaking the relapse cycle, a teaching guide for professionals.* Madison, CT: Psychosocial Press.

DiClemente, C. C. (1993). Changing addictive behaviors: A process perspective. *Current Directions in Psychological Science, 2*(4), 101–106.

Ellis, A. (1988). *How to stubbornly refuse to make yourself miserable about anything—Yes anything!* Secaucus, NJ: Lyle Stuart.

Ellis, A., & Becker, I. (1982). *A guide to personal happiness.* North Hollywood, CA: Wilshire.

Maier, S., Seligman, M., & Solomon, R. (1969). Pavlovian fear conditioning and learned helplessness. In B. A. Campbell & R. M. Church (Eds.), *Punishment* (pp. 299–342). New York: Appleton-Century-Crofts.

Patterson, G. R. (1985). A microsocial analysis of anger and irritable behavior. In M. Chesney & R. Roseman (Eds.), *Anger and hostility in cardiovascular and behavioral disorders* (pp. 83–100). New York: Hemisphere.

Seligman, M. (1975). *Helplessness: On depression, development, and death.* San Francisco: Freeman.

Shapiro, D. (1965). *Neurotic lifestyles.* New York: Basic Books.

Wegscheider-Crus, S. (1976). *The family trap.* St. Paul: Nurturing Network.

Wolf, E. (1988). *Treating the self.* New York: Guilford Press.

CHAPTER 4

The Role of Triggers and Cues in Relapse and Misdirected Anger

Annis, H. (1986). A relapse prevention model for the treatment of alcoholics. In W. Miler & N. Heather (Eds.), *Treating addictive behaviors: Processes of change* (pp. 407–433). New York: Plenum.

Clancy, J. (1996). *Anger and addiction: Breaking the relapse cycle, a teaching guide for professionals.* Madison, CT: Psychosocial Press.

Deschner, J. (1984). *How to end the hitting habit: Anger control for battering couples.* New York: Free Press.

DiClemente, C. C. (1993). Changing addictive behaviors: A process perspective. *Current Directions in Psychological Science, 2*(4), 101–106.

Ellis, A. (1971). *Growth through reason.* Hollywood, CA: Wilshire Books.

Gorski, T., & Miller, M. (1986). *Staying sober: A guide for relapse prevention.* Independence, MO: Independence Press.

Mahoney, M. J., & Thoresen, C. E. (1974). *Self-control: Power to the person.* Monterey, CA: Brooks/Cole.

Marlatt, G. A., & Gordon, J. (Eds.). (1985). *Relapse prevention: A self-control strategy for the maintenance of behavior change.* New York: Guilford Press.

Meichenbaum, D. (1986). Cognitive behavior modification. In F. H. Kanfer & A. P. Goldstein (Eds.), *Helping people change: A textbook of methods* (pp. 346–380). New York: Pergamon Press.

Miller, M., Gorski, T., & Miller, D. K. (1982). *Learning to live again—A guide to recovery from alcoholism.* Independence, MO: Independence Press.

Mueller, A., & Ketcham, K. (1987). *Recovering: How to get and stay sober.* Toronto: Bantam Books.

Potter-Efron, R., & Potter-Efron, P. (1991). *Anger, alcoholism, and addiction: Treating individuals, couples, and families.* New York: W. W. Norton.

Sonkin, D. J., & Durphy, M. (1982). *Learning to live without violence: A handbook for men* (rev. ed.). San Francisco: Volcano Press.

Vaillant, G. E. (1983). *The natural history of alcoholism: Causes, patterns, and paths to recovery.* Cambridge, MA: Harvard University Press.

Walker, L. (1980). *The battered woman syndrome.* New York: Springer.

CHAPTER 5

The Time-Out Technique

Barlow, D. H. (1978). Aversive procedures. In W. S. Agras (Ed.), *Behavior modification: Principles and clinical applications* (2nd ed., pp. 87–125). Boston: Little, Brown.

Clancy, J. (1996). *Anger and addiction: Breaking the relapse cycle, a teaching guide for professionals.* Madison, CT: Psychosocial Press.

Daley, D. (1988). *Relapse prevention.* Bradenton, FL: Human Services Institute.

Deschner, J. (1984). *How to end the hitting habit: Anger control for battering couples.* New York: Free Press.

Hecker, M., & Lunde, D. (1985). On the diagnosis and treatment of chronically hostile individuals. In M. Chesney & R. Roseman (Eds.), *Anger and hostility in cardiovascular and behavioral disorders* (pp. 227–240). New York: Hemisphere.

Potter-Efron, P., & Potter-Efron, R. (1991). Anger as a treatment concern with alcoholics and affected family members. *Alcoholism Treatment Quarterly, 8*(3), 31–46.

Potter-Efron, R., & Potter-Efron, P. (1991). *Anger, alcoholism, and addiction: Treating individuals, couples, and families.* New York: W. W. Norton.

Skinner, B. F. (1948). *Walden II.* New York: Macmillan.

Skinner, B. F. (1971). *Beyond freedom and dignity.* New York: Pocket Books.

Sonkin, J., & Durphy, M. (1982). *Learning to live without violence: A handbook for men* (rev. ed.). San Francisco: Volcano Press.

CHAPTER 6

The Role of Self-Talk in Relapse, Misdirected Anger, and Recovery

Annis, H., & Davis, C. (1987). Assessment of expectancies in alcohol dependent clients. In G. A. Marlatt & D. Donovan (Eds.), *Assessment of addictive behaviors* (pp. 84–111). New York: Guilford Press.

Annis, H., & Davis, C. (1987). Self-efficacy and the prevention of alcoholic relapse: Initial findings from a treatment trial. In T. Baker & D. Cannon (Eds.), *Addictive disorders: Psychological research on assessment and treatment* (pp. 88–112). New York: Praeger.

Beck, A. T. (1976). *Cognitive therapy and emotional disorders*. New York: International Universities Press.

Black, C., & Bucky, S. (1986). Interpersonal and emotional consequences of being an adult child of an alcoholic. *International Journal of Addictions, 21*(2), 213–231.

Clancy, J. (1996). *Anger and addiction: Breaking the relapse cycle, a teaching guide for professionals*. Madison, CT: Psychosocial Press.

Corey, G. (1991). *Theory and practice of counseling and psychotherapy*. New York: Random House.

DiClemente, C. C. (1993). Changing addictive behaviors: A process perspective. *Current Directions in Psychological Science, 2*(4), 101–106.

Ellis, A. (1962). *Reason and emotion in psychotherapy*. New York: Lyle Stuart.

Ellis, A. (1971). *Growth through reason*. Hollywood, CA: Wilshire Books.

Ellis, A. (1973). *Humanistic psychotherapy*. New York: McGraw-Hill.

Ellis, A. (1985). *Overcoming resistance: Rational–emotive therapy with difficult clients*. New York: Springer.

Ellis, A. (1988). *How to stubbornly refuse to make yourself miserable about anything—Yes anything!* Secaucus, NJ: Lyle Stuart.

Gorski, T., & Miller, M. (1986). *Staying sober: A guide for relapse prevention*. Independence, MO: Independence Press.

Marlatt, G. A., & Gordon, J. (Eds.). (1985). *Relapse prevention: A self-control strategy for the maintenance of behavior change*. New York: Guilford Press.

Meichenbaum, D. (1977). *Cognitive behavior modification: An integrative approach*. New York: Plenum.

Meichenbaum, D. (1986). Cognitive behavior modification. In F. H. Kanfer & A. P. Goldstein (Eds.), *Helping people change: A textbook of methods* (pp. 346–380). New York: Pergamon Press.

Potter-Efron, R. (1989). *Shame, guilt, and alcoholism: Treatment issues in clinical practice*. New York: Haworth Press.

Wegscheider, S. (1981). *Another chance: Hope and health for the alcoholic family*. Palo Alto, CA: Science & Behavior Books.

Wegscheider-Crus, S. (1976). *The family trap*. St. Paul: Nurturing Books.

Woititz, J. (1983). *Adult children of alcoholics*. Hollywood, FL: Health Communications.

Wallace, J. (1985). *Alcoholism: New light on the disease*. Warwick, RI: Edgehill Pubns.

CHAPTER 7

Personal Styles of Communication

Annis, H., & Davis, C. (1987). Assessment of expectancies in alcohol dependent clients. In G. A. Marlatt & D. Donovan (Eds.), *Assessment of addictive behaviors* (pp. 84–111). New York: Guilford Press.

Annis, H., & Davis, C. (1987). Self-efficacy and the prevention of alcoholic relapse: Initial findings from a treatment trial. In T. Baker & D. Cannon (Eds.), *Addictive disorders: Psychological research on assessment and treatment* (pp. 88–112). New York: Praeger.

Beck, A. T. (1976). *Cognitive therapy and emotional disorders.* New York: International Universities Press.

Beck, A. (1988). *Love is never enough.* New York: Harper & Row.

Black, C., & Bucky, S. (1986). Interpersonal and emotional consequences of being an adult child of an alcoholic. *International Journal of Addictions, 21*(2), 213–231.

Clancy, J. (1996). *Anger and addiction: Breaking the relapse cycle, a teaching guide for professionals.* Madison, CT: Psychosocial Press.

Daley, D. (1988). *Relapse prevention.* Bradenton, FL: Human Services Institute.

Deschner, J. (1984). *How to end the hitting habit: Anger control for battering couples.* New York: Free Press.

DiClemente, C. C. (1993). Changing addictive behaviors: A process perspective. *Current Directions in Psychological Science, 2*(4), 101–106.

Ellis, A. (1973). *Humanistic psychotherapy.* New York: McGraw-Hill.

Ellis, A. (1985). *Overcoming resistance: Rational–emotive therapy with difficult clients.* New York: Springer.

Ellis, A., & Becker, I. (1982). *A guide to personal happiness.* North Hollywood, CA: Wilshire.

Ellis, A., & Harper, R. A. (1975). *A guide to rational living.* North Hollywood, CA: Wilshire.

Ellis, A., McInerney, J., DiGiuseppe, R., & Yeager, R. (1988). *Rational–emotive therapy with alcoholics and substance abusers.* New York: Pergamon.

Mahoney, M. J., & Thoresen, C. E. (1974). *Self-control: Power to the person.* Monterey, CA: Brooks/Cole.

Marlatt, G. A., & Gordon, J. (Eds.). (1985). *Relapse prevention: A self-control strategy for the maintenance of behavior change.* New York: Guilford Press.

Meichenbaum, D. (1977). *Cognitive behavior modification: An integrative approach.* New York: Plenum.

Meichenbaum, D. (1977). Cognitive behavior modification. In F. H. Kanfer & A. P. Goldstein (Eds.), *Helping people change: A textbook of methods* (pp. 346–380). New York: Pergamon Press.

Sonkin, J., & Durphy, M. (1982). *Learning to live without violence: A handbook for men* (rev. ed.). San Francisco: Volcano Press.

Wegscheider, S. (1981). *Another chance: Hope and health for the alcoholic family.* Palo Alto, CA: Science & Behavior Books.

Wegscheider-Crus, S. (1976). *The family trap.* St. Paul: Nurturing Books.

Woititz, J. (1983). *Adult children of alcoholics.* Hollywood, FL: Health Communications.

CHAPTER 8

Generation Options/Problem Solving

Black, C., & Bucky, S. (1986). Interpersonal and emotional consequences of being an adult child of an alcoholic. *International Journal of Addictions, 21*(2), 213–231.

Clancy, J. (1996). *Anger and addiction: Breaking the relapse cycle, a teaching guide for professionals*. Madison, CT: Psychosocial Press.

Ellis, A. (1962). *Reason and emotion in psychotherapy*. New York: Lyle Stuart.

Ellis, A. (1971). *Growth through reason*. Hollywood, CA: Wilshire Books.

Ellis, A. (1973). *Humanistic psychotherapy*. New York: McGraw-Hill.

Ellis, A. (1985). *Overcoming resistance: Rational–emotive therapy with difficult clients*. New York: Springer.

Ellis, A., & Becker, I. (1982). *A guide to personal happiness*. North Hollywood, CA: Wilshire.

Ellis, A., & Bernard, M. E. (Eds.) (1985). *Clinical applications of rational–emotive therapy*. New York: Plenum.

Ellis, A., & Harper, R. A. (1975). *A guide to rational living*. North Hollywood, CA: Wilshire.

Meichenbaum, D. (1986). Cognitive behavior modification. In F. H. Kanfer & A. P. Goldstein (Eds.), *Helping people change:* A *textbook of methods* (pp. 346–380). New York: Pergamon Press.

Wallace, J. (1985). *Alcoholism: New light on the disease*. Warwick, RI: Edgehill Pubns.

Wegscheider, S. (1981). *Another chance: Hope and health for the alcoholic family*. Palo Alto, CA: Science & Behavior Books.

Wegscheider-Crus, S. (1976). *The family trap*. St. Paul: Nurturing Books.

Woititz, J. (1983). *Adult children of alcoholics*. Hollywood, FL: Health Communications.

CHAPTER 9

Asking for What You Want/Saying No (Limit Setting)

Annis, H. (1986). A relapse prevention model for the treatment of alcoholics. In W. Miler & N. Heather (Eds.), *Treating addictive behaviors: Processes of change* (pp. 407–433). New York: Plenum.

Annis, H., & Davis, C. (1987). Assessment of expectancies in alcohol dependent clients. In G. A. Marlatt & D. Donovan (Eds.), *Assessment of addictive behaviors* (pp. 84–111). New York: Guilford Press.

Annis, H., & Davis, C. (1987). Self-efficacy and the prevention of alcoholic relapse: Initial findings from a treatment trial. In T. Baker & D. Cannon (Eds.), *Addictive disorders: Psychological research on assessment and treatment* (pp. 88–112). New York: Praeger.

Black, C., & Bucky, S. (1986). Interpersonal and emotional consequences of being an adult child of an alcoholic. *International Journal of Addictions, 21*(2), 213–231.

Clancy, J. (1996). *Anger and addiction: Breaking the relapse cycle, a teaching guide for professionals*. Madison, CT: Psychosocial Press.

Daley, D. (1988). *Relapse prevention.* Bradenton, FL: Human Services Institute.

Ellis, A., McInerney, J., DiGiuseppe, R., & Yeager, R. (1988). *Rational–emotive therapy with alcoholics and substance abusers.* New York: Pergamon.

Gorski, T., & Miller, M. (1986). *Staying sober: A guide for relapse prevention.* Independence, MO: Independence Press.

Marlatt, G. A., & Gordon, J. (Eds.). (1985). *Relapse prevention: A self-control strategy for the maintenance of behavior change.* New York: Guilford Press.

Meichenbaum, D. (1986). Cognitive behavior modification. In F. H. Kanfer & A. P. Goldstein (Eds.), *Helping people change: A textbook of methods* (pp. 346–380). New York: Pergamon Press.

Mueller, A., & Ketcham, K. (1987). *Recovering: How to get and stay sober.* Toronto: Bantam Books.

Potter-Efron, R. (1989). *Shame, guilt, and alcoholism: Treatment issues in clinical practice.* New York: Haworth Press.

Potter-Efron, P., & Potter-Efron, R. (1991). Anger as a treatment concern with alcoholics and affected family members. *Alcoholism Treatment Quarterly, 8*(3), 31–46.

Potter-Efron, R., & Potter-Efron, P. (1991). *Anger, alcoholism, and addiction: Treating individuals, couples, and families.* New York: W. W. Norton.

Wegscheider, S. (1981). *Another chance: Hope and health for the alcoholic family.* Palo Alto, CA: Science & Behavior Books.

Wegscheider-Crus, S. (1976). *The family trap.* St. Paul: Nurturing Books.

Woititz, J. (1983). *Adult children of alcoholics.* Hollywood, FL: Health Communications.

CHAPTER 10

Stress and the Anger–Relapse Cycle

Clancy, J. (1996). *Anger and addiction: Breaking the relapse cycle, a teaching guide for professionals.* Madison, CT: Psychosocial Press.

Daley, D. (1988). *Relapse prevention.* Bradenton, FL: Human Services Institute.

Gorski, T., & Miller, M. (1986). *Staying sober: A guide for relapse prevention.* Independence, MO: Independence Press.

Marlatt, G. A., & Gordon, J. (Eds.). (1985). *Relapse prevention: A self-control strategy for the maintenance of behavior change.* New York: Guilford Press.

Munz, D. (1983). *Stress management participant's manual.* St. Louis: St. Louis University Health Center—Healthline.

Seyle, H. (1956). *The stress of life.* New York: McGraw-Hill.

Seyle, H. (1974). *Stress without distress.* Philadelphia: Lippincott.

CHAPTER 11

Stress Management

Beck, A. T. (1976). *Cognitive therapy and emotional disorders.* New York: International Universities Press.

Beck, A. (1988). *Love is never enough.* New York: Harper & Row.

Clancy, J. (1996). *Anger and addiction: Breaking the relapse cycle, a teaching guide for professionals.* Madison, CT: Psychosocial Press.

Ellis, A. (1962). *Reason and emotion in psychotherapy.* New York: Lyle Stuart.

Ellis, A. (1971). *Growth through reason.* Hollywood, CA: Wilshire Books.

Ellis, A. (1973). *Humanistic psychotherapy.* New York: McGraw-Hill.

Ellis, A. (1977). Fun in psychotherapy. *Rational Living, 12*(1), 2–6.

Ellis, A. (1985). *Overcoming resistance: Rational–emotive therapy with difficult clients.* New York: Springer.

Ellis, A. (1987). The use of rational humorous songs in psychotherapy. In W. F. Fry, Jr., & W. A. Salemeh (Eds.), *Handbook of humor and psychotherapy* (pp. 265–287). Sarasota, FL: Professional Resource Exchange.

Ellis, A. (1988). *How to stubbornly refuse to make yourself miserable about anything—Yes anything!* Secaucus, NJ: Lyle Stuart.

Ellis, A., & Harper, R. A. (1975). *A guide to rational living.* North Hollywood, CA: Wilshire.

Ellis, A., McInerney, J., DiGiuseppe, R., & Yeager, R. (1988). *Rational–emotive therapy with alcoholics and substance abusers.* New York: Pergamon.

Ketcham, K., & Mueller, L. A. (1985). *Eating right to live sober.* Rotan, TX: Madrona Pubs.

Meichenbaum, D. (1986). Cognitive behavior modification. In F. H. Kanfer & A. P. Goldstein (Eds.), *Helping people change: A textbook of methods* (pp. 346–380). New York: Pergamon Press.

Milam, J., & Ketcham, K. (1981). *Under the influence: A guide to the myths and realities of alcoholism.* Seattle: Madrona.

Miller, M., Gorski, T., & Miller, D. K. (1982). *Learning to live again—A guide to recovery from alcoholism.* Independence, MO: Independence Press.

Mueller, A., & Ketcham, K. (1987). *Recovering: How to get and stay sober.* Toronto: Bantam Books.

CHAPTER 12

Resentment, Misdirected Anger, and Relapse

Abramson, L., Seligman, M., & Teasdale, J. (1978). Learned helplessness in humans: Critique and reformulation. *Journal of Abnormal Psychology, 87,* 49–74.

Black, C., & Bucky, S. (1986). Interpersonal and emotional consequences of being an adult child of an alcoholic. *International Journal of Addictions, 21*(2), 213–231.

Bootzin, R. (1980). *Abnormal psychology* (3rd ed.). New York: Random House.

Clancy, J. (1996). *Anger and addiction: Breaking the relapse cycle, a teaching guide for professionals.* Madison, CT: Psychosocial Press.

Daley, D. (1988). *Relapse prevention.* Bradenton, FL: Human Services Institute.

Ellis, A., & Becker, I. (1982). *A guide to personal happiness.* North Hollywood, CA: Wilshire.

Ellis, A., & Harper, R.A. (1975). *A guide to rational living.* North Hollywood, CA: Wilshire.

Gorski, T., & Miller, M. (1986). *Staying sober: A guide for relapse prevention.* Independence, MO: Independence Press.

Maier, S., Seligman, M., & Solomon, R. (1969). Pavlovian fear conditioning and learned helplessness. In B. A. Campbell & R. M. Church (Eds.), *Punishment* (pp. 299–342). New York: Appleton-Century-Crofts.

Potter-Efron, R. (1989). *Shame, guilt, and alcoholism: Treatment issues in clinical practice.* New York: Haworth Press.

Potter-Efron, R., & Potter-Efron, P. (1989). *Letting go of shame: Understanding shame in our lives.* Center City, MN: Hazeldon/Harper & Row.

Potter-Efron, P., & Potter-Efron, R. (1991). Anger as a treatment concern with alcoholics and affected family members. *Alcoholism Treatment Quarterly, 8*(3), 31–46.

Potter-Efron, R., & Potter-Efron, P. (1991). *Anger, alcoholism, and addiction: Treating individuals, couples, and families.* New York: W. W. Norton.

Potter-Efron, R., & Potter-Efron, P. (1991). *Ending our resentments.* Center City, MN: Hazeldon Press.

Seligman, M. (1975). *Helplessness: On depression, development, and death.* San Francisco: Freeman.

Smedes, L. (1984). *Forgive and forget.* New York: Pocket Books.

Wegscheider, S. (1981). *Another chance: Hope and health for the alcoholic family.* Palo Alto, CA: Science & Behavior Books.

Wegscheider-Crus, S. (1976). *The family trap.* St. Paul: Nurturing Books.

Wolf, E. (1988). *Treating the self.* New York: Guilford Press.

Woititz, J. (1983). *Adult children of alcoholics.* Hollywood, FL: Health Communications.

CHAPTER 13

Reinforcing New Relapse Prevention Skills

Annis, H. (1986). A relapse prevention model for the treatment of alcoholics. In W. Miler & N. Heather, (Eds.), *Treating addictive behaviors: Processes of change* (pp. 407–433). New York: Plenum.

Annis, H., & Davis, C. (1987). Assessment of expectancies in alcohol dependent clients. In G. A. Marlatt & D. Donovan (Eds.), *Assessment of addictive behaviors* (pp. 88–112). New York: Guilford Press.

Bandura, A. (1969). *Principles of behavior modification.* New York: Holt, Rinehart & Winston.

Bandura, A. (1971). *Psychological modeling: Conflict theories.* Chicago: Aldine-Atherton.

Barlow, D. H. (1978). Aversive procedures. In W. S. Agras (Ed.), *Behavior modification: Principles and clinical applications* (2nd ed., pp. 87–125). Boston: Little, Brown.

Beck, A. T. (1976). *Cognitive therapy and emotional disorders.* New York: International Universities Press.

Beck, A. (1988). *Love is never enough.* New York: Harper & Row.

Clancy, J. (1996). *Anger and addiction: Breaking the relapse cycle, a teaching guide for professionals.* Madison, CT: Psychosocial Press.

Daley, D. (1988). *Relapse prevention.* Bradenton, FL: Human Services Institute.

Ellis, A. (1973). *Humanistic psychotherapy.* New York: McGraw-Hill.
Ellis, A. (1985). *Overcoming resistance: Rational–emotive therapy with difficult clients.* New York: Springer.
Ellis, A., & Becker, I. (1982). *A guide to personal happiness.* North Hollywood, CA: Wilshire.
Ellis, A., & Harper, R. A. (1975). *A guide to rational living.* North Hollywood, CA: Wilshire.
Ellis, A., McInerney, J., DiGiuseppe, R., & Yeager, R. (1988). *Rational–emotive therapy with alcoholics and substance abusers.* New York: Pergamon.
Gorski, T., & Miller, M. (1986). *Staying sober: A guide for relapse prevention.* Independence, MO: Independence Press.
Mahoney, M. J. (1974). *Cognition and behavior modification.* Cambridge, MA: Ballinger.
Mahoney, M. J., & Thoresen, C. E. (1974). *Self-control: Power to the person.* Monterey, CA: Brooks/Cole.
Marlatt, G. A., & Gordon, J. (Eds.). (1985). *Relapse prevention: A self-control strategy for the maintenance of behavior change.* New York: Guilford Press.
Meichenbaum, D. (1986). Cognitive behavior modification. In F. H. Kanfer & A. P. Goldstein (Eds.), *Helping people change: A textbook of methods* (pp. 346–380). New York: Pergamon Press.

CHAPTER 14

Twelve-Step Recovery

Anonymous (1976). *Alcoholics anonymous: The story of how many thousands of men and women have recovered from alcoholism* (3rd ed.). New York: Alcoholics Anonymous World Services.